BIOWARFARE AND TERRORISM

BIOWARFARE
AND
TERRORISM

by

Francis A. Boyle

CLARITY PRESS, INC.

© 2005 Francis A. Boyle
ISBN: 0-932863-46-9

In-house editor: Diana G. Collier

Cover photo: Envelope containing anthrax sent to Senator Daschle
AP/World Wide Photos.
Note: "Fort Detrick, Maryland, USA"
did not appear on the original envelope.

ALL RIGHTS RESERVED: Except for purposes of review, this book may not be copied, or stored in any information retrieval system, in whole or in part, without permission in writing from the publishers.

Also by Francis A. Boyle:
World Politics and International Law (1985)
Defending Civil Resistance under International Law (1987)
The Future of International Law and American Foreign Policy
(1989)
The Bosnian People Charge Genocide (1996)
Foundations of World Order (1999)
The Criminality of Nuclear Deterrence (2002)
Palestine, Palestinians and International Law (2003)
Destroying World Order (2004)

Library of Congress Cataloging-in-Publication Data

Boyle, Francis Anthony, 1950-
Biowarfare and terrorism / by Francis A. Boyle ; foreword by Jonathan King.
p. cm.
Includes bibliographical references and index.
ISBN 0-932863-46-9
1. Biological warfare. 2. Biological warfare—United States. 3. Bioterrorism. 4. Biological weapons. 5. Biological weapons—United States. 6. Biological arms control. 7. Militarism—United States. I. Title.
UG447.8.B75 2005
358'.38—dc22

2005024557

CLARITY PRESS, INC.
Ste. 469, 3277 Roswell Rd. NE
Atlanta, GA. 30305
http://www.claritypress.com

TABLE OF CONTENTS

FOREWORD by Jonathan King / 11

CALL FOR A BAN ON THE GENETIC ALTERATION OF
PATHOGENS FOR DESTRUCTIVE PURPOSES / 15

INTRODUCTION / 17

CHAPTER ONE:
THE BIOLOGICAL WEAPONS CONVENTION / 19
Origins of the BWC Convention / 19
The BWC Loophole / 20
The Reaganite Neo-Cons / 21

CHAPTER TWO:
MAKING BIOLOGICAL WEAPONS / 23
Stages of the Biological Weapons-Making Process / 23

CHAPTER THREE:
U.S. GOVERNMENT BIOWARFARE CONTRACTS / 25
Biowarfare Research at the University of Illinois,
    Urbana-Champaign Campus / 26
American Universities Line Up at the BDRP Trough / 26
Shaky Scientific Ethics a Biowarfare Problem? / 27
The Need for Appropriate Biowarfare Contract Review / 28

CHAPTER FOUR:
THE BIOLOGICAL WEAPONS
ANTI-TERRORISM ACT OF 1989 / 29
The Biotechnology Industry Changes Course / 30
Governmental Resistance to Regulating Biowarfare
    Research / 31
The Neo-Cons under Reagan Violate the Biological
    Weapons Convention / 32

The Bush Sr. Administration Acts Responsibly on
    Biowarfare / 33
Primary Features of the Biological Weapons
    Anti-Terrorism Act / 34
Closing the Door on Biowarfare Research Loopholes / 37

CHAPTER FIVE:
U.S. BIOWARFARE-RELATED VIOLATIONS
OF INTERNATIONAL LAW / 39
Iraq: The Nuremberg Code on Medical Experimentation / 39
The Clinton Administration Violates the Biological
    Weapons Convention / 41
The George W. Bush Administration Repudiates the
    Verification Protocol of the BWC / 42

CHAPTER SIX:
DOMESTIC TERRORISM: THE ANTHRAX ATTACKS ON
THE U.S. CONGRESS / 44
The FBI Cover-Up: Motivating Factors / 46
Resounding Silence / 48
Linkage Between the Anthrax Attacks and 9/11? / 49

CHAPTER SEVEN:
GEARING UP TO FIGHT AND "WIN" BIOWARFARE / 53
WMD Partnering: Nuclear and Bioweaponry / 54
PNAC Bombshell a Harbinger? / 55
The Bush Jr. Administration's Plans for Bio-WMD
    Wars of Aggression / 56
Bush Undersecretary of State for Arms Control—
    Gung Ho for Bios / 58
To Fight and "Win" by Biowarfare: The Prerequisites / 58
The Smoking Gun: The Pentagon's Chemical and
    Biological Defense Program / 59
The Offensive Nature of "Civilian Defense" / 64
More Criminal Exposure for the CBDP / 66
Can World War III Be Far Behind? / 72
Bush Jr.'s Banana Republic / 72

CHAPTER EIGHT:
REINING IN BIOWARFARE RESEARCH:

HOW IT CAN BE DONE / WHY WE MUST DO IT / 75
No Escape for U.S. in Misinterpreting BWC
    Obligations / 75
Activating the Biological Weapons Convention's
    Complaint Procedure / 78
Filing a BWC Complaint for Investigation by the U.N.
    Secretary-General / 81
Hoisting the Bush Jr. Administration With Its Own
    Petard / 82
Further Recourse Through the U.N. General
    Assembly / 85
A Warning to Scientists / 86
Campaign for the Peaceful Development of the
    Biological Sciences / 87
A Letter of Demand to the Department of Defense
    on the CBDP Final Programmatic Environmental
    Impact Statement
    by Francis A. Boyle and Terry J. Lodge / 91

CONCLUSION / 108

APPENDIX I
CRITIQUE OF THE PENTAGON'S BIOLOGICAL
DEFENSE RESEARCH PROGRAM (1988) / 112

APPENDIX II
BIOWARFARE RESEARCH AT THE UNIVERSITY OF
ILLINOIS COLLEGE OF VETERINARY MEDICINE / 122

APPENDIX III
PROTOCOL FOR THE PROHIBITION OF THE USE IN
WAR OF ASPHYXIATING, POISONOUS OR OTHER
GASES, AND OF BACTERIOLOGICAL METHODS OF
WARFARE / 124

APPENDIX IV
CONVENTION ON THE PROHIBITION OF THE DEVELOP-
MENT, PRODUCTION AND STOCKPILING OF BACTERIO-
LOGICAL (BIOLOGICAL) AND TOXIN WEAPONS AND ON
THEIR DESTRUCTION / 126

ENDNOTES / 133

INDEX / 140

Dedication

In Honor of Richard C. Lewontin:
Teacher, Mentor, and Friend

I wish to express my deep gratitude to my Common Core Biology Sequence teachers at the University of Chicago during the 1969—1970 academic year, whose superb instruction made the work described herein possible: Lorna Strauss (Biochemistry); Richard C. Lewontin (Population Biology); and Bernard Strauss (Genetics). In particular, the courage, integrity, and principles of Dick Lewontin have always been a tremendous source of inspiration and guidance to me from the very outset of my career in higher education. I shall always fondly regret that I could not continue working with him. So I dedicate this book to Richard C. Lewontin, Alexander Agassiz Professor of Zoology and Biology at Harvard University, now Emeritus: Stolat! Nevertheless, I alone am solely responsible for its contents.

F.A.B.

CALL FOR A BAN ON THE GENETIC ALTERATION OF PATHOGENS FOR DESTRUCTIVE PURPOSES

3 November 2001
Harvard Divinity School
Cambridge, MA 02138

The recent use of the US Postal Service to disseminate anthrax-contaminated mail underscores a more general threat to people worldwide brought about by the perversion of the biological sciences to cause harm through the deliberate spread of disease.* This is the moment to outlaw all destructive applications of genetic engineering.

We call on the United States to immediately halt all projects designed to genetically modify naturally occurring organisms for military purposes.

We call on the States Parties to the 1972 Biological Weapons Convention to extend the Convention's ban to cover all genetic modification of biological agents for military purposes. Since the line between offense and defense in this context is thin to non-existent, there should be no loopholes for "defense." Genetic modification of pathogens for development of vaccines or other medical purposes should be carried out in civilian laboratories and under strict international controls.

Finally, we call on the United States to support a Protocol to the Biological Weapons Convention to assure strict compliance with the terms of the Convention both by states and by individuals and sub-state organizations.

Signed,

Francis A. Boyle, Professor of International Law at University of Illinois College of Law, author of U.S. implementing legislation for 1972 Biological Weapons Convention, the Biological Weapons Anti-Terrorism Act of 1989.

Jonathan King, PhD, Professor of Molecular Biology at the Massachusetts Institute of Technology and Director of the Biology Electron Microscope Facility.

Martin Teitel, PhD, President of the Council for Responsible Genetics.

Susan Wright, PhD, Associate Research Scientist at the University of Michigan.

*Several developed countries, including the United States, have initiated projects aimed at genetically engineering pathogenic and other microbes for military purposes. Military-sponsored projects include:

1) developing "superbugs" capable of digesting materials such as plastics, fuel, rubber, and asphalt;

2) developing a strain of anthrax that overcomes the protection provided by vaccines in the name of "defense" against such genetically altered strains.

These projects are being justified under the terms of the Biological Weapons Convention as necessary for "defense." Far from providing defense, these projects open up the possibility of more dangerous forms of biological warfare against which there is no defense. They also undermine the Convention both because the actual motives for these projects are highly ambiguous (if a country were to withdraw from the Biological Weapons Convention, their projects would have direct offensive applications) and because they will stimulate similar projects elsewhere in the world.

INTRODUCTION

Starting in October of 2001, the world witnessed terrorist anthrax attacks on the American government that were obviously designed to shut down the U.S. Congress at a very critical moment in America's history as a Republic, that is, immediately after the terrorist attacks of September 11. It was during this precise moment that Congress should have been in session, making vital decisions, exercising strict oversight of the executive branch of government, and in particular the White House under President George W. Bush, the Department of Justice under Attorney General John Ashcroft, the Department of Defense under Secretary of Defense Donald Rumsfeld, and the Central Intelligence Agency under Director George Tenet. Such U.S. congressional oversight did not occur because of these terrorist anthrax attacks. Even worse yet, President Bush and Attorney General Ashcroft deviously manipulated these terrorist anthrax attacks on Congress in order to stampede the American people and the U.S. Congress into enacting into law the totalitarian U.S.A. Patriot Act with almost no congressional input whatsoever.

This book will discuss some of the historical background for the law, the policy, and the science behind biological weapons in the United States: how and why the United States government initiated, sustained, and then dramatically expanded an illegal biological arms race with potentially catastrophic consequences for the human species and its supporting biosphere on this fragile planet Earth.

By contextualizing the politico-legal and scientific environment in which this historic first biowarfare terrorist attack against the U.S. government—the anthrax attacks on Congress of 2001—took place, this book also seeks to shed new light on these disquieting questions: Why did this unprecedented event disappear so swiftly from public media discussion? Why has the FBI search for the perpetrators lost steam? Why has Congress itself failed to pursue both the specific instance and the ramifications of this terrorist attack upon it, and the failure to find a perpetrator? Why has there been no outcry at that failure? For what reasons might the true perpetrators never be found?

In light of the Bush administration's recent expansion of funding for "biological defense" research, including proposed testing on human subjects, and the evident and now demonstrated threat biowarfare poses not just to the American public but to humanity as a whole, this book provides a politico-legal guide on how to arrest the determination of successive American administrations to open the biowarfare Pandora's box.

CHAPTER ONE

THE BIOLOGICAL WEAPONS CONVENTION

Origins of the BWC Convention

The United States has had an extremely aggressive, offensive biological warfare program dating back to World War II, whose full history I will not recount here.[1] To make a long story short, in 1969 President Richard Nixon decided to terminate this program for reasons of Machiavellian realpolitik. First, it was felt that biological weapons were counterproductive militarily because they were difficult to control and thus there could easily be "blowback" on U.S. armed forces in the field as well as upon the American civilian population back at home. Second, the U.S. already possessed a massive and overwhelming arsenal in all categories of nuclear weapons and their related delivery systems, whereas biological weapons were perceived to be the "poor man's atom bomb." Nixon wanted to eliminate these "bios" in order to prevent Third World countries from acquiring access to comparatively inexpensive weapons of mass destruction (WMD). A Biological Weapons Convention prohibiting "bios" would enable the nuclear weapons states of the world to maintain, consolidate and further extend their near-monopoly on WMD that had just been codified by the 1968 Treaty on the Non-Proliferation of Nuclear Weapons.[2] This same perverse Machiavellian calculation would much later lead these same nuclear weapons states to support the negotiation, conclusion and ratification of the 1993 Convention on the Prohibition of the Development, Production, Stockpiling and Use of Chemical Weapons and on Their Destruction.[3]

Starting in 1969, President Nixon unilaterally ordered the destruction of U.S. anti-personnel biological agents and munitions, a process that was ostensibly completed as of early 1973.[4] Nevertheless, despite the President's order, the CIA continued to research and develop biological weapons.[5] Eventually the United States supported the negotiation, conclusion and ratification of the Convention on the Prohibition of the Development, Production and Stockpiling of Bacteriological (Biological) and Toxin Weapons and on Their Destruction of 1972, which entered into force on 26 March 1975 (hereinafter referred to as the BWC),[6] which is reprinted in Appendix IV.

The BWC Loophole

Article I of the BWC obligates the state contracting parties "never in any circumstances to develop, produce, stockpile or otherwise acquire or retain:

> (1) Microbial or other biological agents, or toxins whatever their origin or method of production, of types and in quantities that have no justification for prophylactic, protective or other peaceful purposes;
>
> (2) Weapons, equipment or means of delivery designed to use such agents or toxins for hostile purposes or in armed conflict."

Notice BWC article I does not prohibit "research" for "prophylactic, protective or other peaceful purposes." This became the proverbial exception that the United States government exploited in order to nullify the general rule of "bios" prohibition found in BWC article I.[7] Notice also that the BWC does not *in haec verba* prohibit the "use" of biological weapons in warfare. That prohibition had already been previously established by the 1925 Geneva Protocol, reprinted here in Appendix III. Nevertheless, according to the Preamble to the BWC, the states parties to the convention basically incorporated by reference the Protocol's prohibition on the use of biological weapons in warfare:

> Reaffirming their adherence to the principles and objectives of that Protocol and calling upon all States to comply strictly with them.

To its great credit, during the Nixon administration the U.S. government eventually did wind down its offensive biological warfare program. But most ominously there lurked in the bowels of the Pentagon the remnants of the old Chemical and Biological Warfare (CBW) Unit waiting, wishing, hoping, planning, and scheming to spring back into life. In retrospect, this was one bureaucratic vampire that should have had a budgetary stake driven through its heart by Congress in order to kill it off once and for all time.

The Reaganite Neo-Cons

Then in 1981 the Reagan administration came to power, staffed with many of its self-styled Neo-conservative operatives, who were embedded at the Pentagon. Two decades later, many of these same Neo-Con apparatchiks returned to power with the advent of the Bush Jr. administration in 2001, and then received bureaucratic promotions for their past nefarious services rendered.[8] The Reaganites took the position that America would exploit its technological superiority in all fields of scientific endeavor across the board for war-related purposes: nuclear, chemical, biological, space, lasers, computers, etc.[9] So the Reaganites began to pour massive amounts of money into researching and developing biological agents for what they alleged to be "defensive" purposes.[10]

Despite popular misconceptions to the contrary, BWC article I does not create an exception for "defense," or "deterrence," let alone "retaliation," but only for "prophylactic, protective or other peaceful purposes."[11] Those who supported the BWC were only too aware that "defense" is not necessarily "peaceful." As if in illustration of that very reality, the Reaganite Neo-Cons, fervently believing in the Machiavellian principle that "the best defense is a good offense," proceeded to act accordingly, *inter alia* on "bios". That same Machiavellian calculus holds true for the Bush Jr. Neo-Cons with respect to their doctrines on waging (allegedly preventative) wars of aggression and their first-use of WMD, including "bios," which will be discussed in more detail below.

In terms of constant dollars, the Reagan administration expended as much money on allegedly "defensive" biowarfare research as the Nixon administration did when the United States government had an overtly offensive and aggressive biowarfare program.[12] In particular, the Reaganites sought to vigorously exploit the U.S. technological superiority in DNA genetic engineering research that had come to the forefront of the life-sciences after the conclusion of the BWC, which therefore had not been drafted to take into specific account the phenomenon of "gene-splicing" for the purpose of developing bioweapons.[13] From the perspective of the BWC, the problem presented by DNA genetic engineering was and still is that it is inherently and unavoidably dual-use–it can be put to both offensive uses and defensive uses at the same time. The biotechnology is exactly the same in either case.

CHAPTER TWO

MAKING BIOLOGICAL WEAPONS

Stages of the Biological Weapons-Making Process

In order to develop a biological weapon, a government needs three basic component units:[14]

(1) A deleterious biological agent.

(2) A vaccine to inoculate its own troops and civilian population in order to protect them from "blowback" by the biological agent its "life-scientists" have developed.

(3) An effective delivery device and dispersal mechanism for the biological agent.

The process works like this. By means of DNA genetic engineering, so-called "life-scientists" develop a novel offensive biological agent. Then, using the precise same gene-splicing biotechnology, these "life-scientists" develop the vaccine. They cap their work by aerosolizing the biological agent and then testing it on living organisms in order to prove that it can be delivered to its intended target with the planned deleterious effects. Finally, these "life-scientists" then turn these three component units of their new and tested biological weapon over to their government for production, stockpiling, and ultimately for deployment and use. Notice that at this point, these "life-scientists" have progressed from what is only arguably exempted "research" into clearly prohibited "development" of "bios" in violation of BWC article I.

As a general proposition, one obvious tip-off that a government biowarfare contract is for illegal, prohibited, and offensive purposes is that it specifically requires the successful aerosolization of the biological agent that is the subject of the contract. This is critical to the success of the new biowarfare weapon because most anti-human biowarfare agents are delivered to their intended victims by air.[15]

In the hands of an unscrupulous government, DNA genetic engineering can easily be manipulated and abused in order to circumvent, nullify and otherwise render obsolete the BWC under the guise of conducting exempted "research" that it unilaterally proclaimed to be "defensive."

This is exactly what the Reaganite Neo-Cons proceeded to do. The Reaganite Pentagon went out and proceeded to contract with researchers at reputable universities all over the United States in order to conduct such dual-use, simultaneously offensive-defensive DNA genetic engineering projects for every exotic disease that could possibly be obtained from nature under the Orwellian name of the "Biological Defense Research Program (BDRP)."[16]

The Bush Jr. Neo-Cons are doing the exact same thing today under the rubric of the Pentagon's so-called Chemical and Biological Defense Program (CBDP), the direct successor to the BDRP.

CHAPTER THREE

U.S. GOVERNMENT BIOWARFARE CONTRACTS

By the late 1980s, it became patently obvious that scientists at many American universities or working for U.S. government laboratories were abusing DNA genetic engineering (1) to develop an offensive biological agent; (2) then an allegedly "defensive" vaccine; (3) aerosolizing the agent; (4) testing the aerosolized agent to make sure it killed animals akin to human beings such as pigs; and then (5) turning the products of their "research" and "development" over to the Pentagon.[17] In other words, these despicable death-scientists were arming the Pentagon with the component units necessary to produce a massive array of DNA genetically engineered biological weapons. From there the Pentagon could easily produce, stockpile, deploy, and use biological weapons in further breach of BWC article I.

At the request of the Council for Responsible Genetics, I submitted a line-by-line analysis of the Reaganite BDRP to the Pentagon by means of a detailed *Memorandum of Law* dated 5 August 1988, which was then published by Transnational Publishers in Chapter 8 of my book, *The Future of International Law and American Foreign Policy* (1989). This analysis is included in Appendix I of this book, with a view to demonstrating that the issues addressed in the contemporary Critique to the CBDP Final Programmatic Environmental Impact Statement of 2004 provided by myself and attorney Terry Lodge (see below) reflect an ongoing and indeed, entrenched, orientation of the DoD over several decades.

Biowarfare Research at the University of Illinois Urbana-Champaign Campus

It became quite clear to me when I obtained and read some of these BDRP contracts let out here at the University of Illinois on the Urbana-Champaign campus, that these scientists actually knew that they were engaged in the development of offensive biowarfare weapons, despite their public protestations to the contrary. Furthermore, these BDRP contracts had been vetted and approved by the University of Illinois' campus-wide "Ethics Committee," whose appointed task is to ensure that ethical standards are applied to contracts involving scientific experiments on animals.[18]

The imprimatur of the Ethics Committee proved to be meaningless. Large numbers of pigs and other animals were hideously gassed to death by means of these aerosolized bio-agents in order to prove to the Pentagon that their related biowarfare weapons worked effectively, and thus fulfill the requirements of these BDRP contracts. For further insight into the issues surrounding this research project, no doubt typical of BDRP and now CBDP in their flimsy pretexts, lack of legitimate justification, and cause of heinous suffering to animals, see Appendix II and Appendix I.

American Universities Line Up at the BDRP Trough

The approval of these BDRP contracts by the University of Illinois' "Ethics Committee" proved how worthless such in-house university ethics committees usually are. Too much money is at stake in these government contracts for any university to have their cherry-picked "ethics" committees reject them. After I had publicly blown the whistle on these BDRP contracts and on other unethical government contracts on campus involving the CIA, we organized a public debate on their academic propriety.[19] The University of Illinois sent in an official representative to defend the contracts. In guise of so doing, that representative publicly admitted that the University of Illinois itself directly takes 51% of every outside research contract dollar under the fictitious accounting guise of "overhead."

To put it bluntly: the University of Illinois and its hand-picked "Ethics Committees" had a vested economic interest in approving unethical if not illegal scientific "research" contracts to be conducted on campus that involve scientific experimentation on animals and human beings, and in this specific case the gruesome torturing to death of our fellow sentient living beings. I suspect the same is true at most other university campuses around the country today. The same principles hold true for the federally-mandated Institutional Biosafety Committees at American Universities, private biotech companies, and U.S. government labs that are supposed to supervise the safety of recombinant-DNA research projects.[20]

American universities have a long history of willingly permitting their research agendas, researchers, institutes, and laboratories to be co-opted, corrupted, and perverted by the Pentagon and the CIA.[21] To what extent is this due to the fact that succeeding U.S. presidential administrations have so cooked the options by allocation of funding, that scientists feel they have little recourse? Reflecting protest within the scientific community at this distortion of research priorities, more than 750 of the nation's leading microbiological researchers have openly called on the Bush Jr. administration to return the nation's scientific focus to more basic pathogens, contending that the shift in emphasis to "biodefense" spending represented a "misdirection" of priorities that has caused a "crisis" in microbiological research. The signatories include at least five past presidents of the American Society for Microbiology and the current acting president.[22]

Shaky Scientific Ethics a Biowarfare Problem?

Furthermore, according to a recent scientific survey of 7,760 scientists funded by the National Institutes of Health (NIH), 38% of the mid-career respondents and 28% of the early-career respondents, for a sum total of 33% of all respondents, admitted that they had engaged in at least one of ten ethically "sanctionable" behaviors during the previous three years.[23] In other words, about one out of every three life scientists are "unethical" in accordance with their own respective judgments of their own work. I suspect that this percentage will increase now that large-numbers of less-qualified life scientists are being seduced into doing biowarfare work by the enormous sums of money being dangled before their eyes by the Bush Jr. administration. In any event, on the basis of this study we can expect that at least one-third of all the magnitudinally increasing biowarfare work performed in the future will be "unethical" to begin with in accordance with the standards adopted by scientists themselves. The illegality and criminality of this biowarfare work are discussed elsewhere in this book.

The Need for Appropriate Biowarfare Contract Review

Consider the scope of this issue. As indicated above, all over America, scientists are converging on the rich feeding trough now made available by the government of President George W. Bush. Not only American universities, but also universities overseas, are succumbing to the financial incentives that these projects provide. Despite the admirable effort of the 750 scientists mentioned above, on the whole, far from acting as a brake on the process, a preponderant number of individual scientists are all too likely to become co-opted into the act.

Who is institutionally empowered to speak for the public interest here? Who guards the guardians? Why are the foxes put in charge of guarding the hen houses? Why is an issue of such consequence to humanity at large, present and future, being carried out in the regulatory equivalent of the Wild West?

In an almost inevitable future biological warfare catastrophe, where would we pinpoint the moment that the dogs of biowarfare were let out?

CHAPTER FOUR

THE BIOLOGICAL WEAPONS ANTI-TERRORISM ACT OF 1989

In response to the wholesale prostitution and degradation of the life-sciences by the Pentagon and BDRP contractors at American universities, the Council for Responsible Genetics (CRG) conducted a Congressional Briefing at Capitol Hill on 13 September 1985. The CRG asked me to speak in order to explain what the Reaganite Neo-Cons really were up to; how dangerous and illegal the proliferation of this biowarfare technology really was; and what could be done to stop it. At the conclusion of my remarks, I called for the drafting and passage of domestic implementing legislation for the Biological Weapons Convention that would make it a serious federal crime in order to stop this dual-use, simultaneously offensive-defensive biowarfare research and development.

By that time, U.S. domestic implementing legislation for the BWC was then long overdue. As required by BWC article IV:

> Each State Party to this Convention shall, in accordance with its constitutional processes, take any necessary measures to prohibit and prevent the development, production, stockpiling, acquisition, or retention of the

> agents, toxins, weapons, equipment and
> means of delivery specified in article I of the
> Convention, within the territory of such State,
> under its jurisdiction or under its control
> anywhere.

Predictably, since it was my suggestion, the CRG then asked me to draft this legislation and in particular to deal with the abuse of DNA genetic engineering technology for biowarfare purposes.[24] On this project I worked in conjunction with our CRG life-scientists (the best in the world!)[25] and with the biotechnology industry.

The Biotechnology Industry Changes Course

Back in the early 1980s, the biotechnology industry had no desire to get involved with "researching" biowarfare technology. As the biotechnology industry saw it then, the real money was to be made in genetically modified (GM) food, not biowarfare. Getting involved in biowarfare research would only detract from their public image and thus undercut their public relations campaign for the acceptance of GM food by the American people.

So the biotech industry supported our CRG draft implementing legislation for the BWC. Sadly, two decades later, after 11 September 2001 and the related terrorist anthrax attacks on the U.S. Congress, the massive amounts of governmental funds devoted to biowarfare development by the Bush Jr. administration were to successfully co-opt and divert the U.S. biotech industry towards biowarfare purposes.[26] According to Rutgers University molecular biologist Richard H. Ebright, over 300 scientific institutes and 12,000 individuals today have access to pathogens suitable for biowarfare and terrorism, with an increasing number of researchers having no prior experience in this area.[27] Furthermore, according to him, the number of N.I.H. grants for researching infectious diseases with biowarfare potential has shot up from 33 in the five years preceding 2001, to 497 since then.[28] According to a recent report by the Centers for Disease

Control and Prevention, only 64 percent of epidemiologists engaged in bioterrorism work have degrees in epidemiology, and 20 percent have no formal training in that field.[29] Those already frightening numbers will exponentially increase now that the U.S. Congress has funded $5.6 billion over the next ten years on Project BioShield alone, among other dangerous bioterrorism boondoggles that will be discussed in more detail below. And now the United States government and Congress are trying to buy off and divert the gargantuan pharmaceutical industry into its biowarfare industry by means of the proposed BioShield II legislation that was introduced into Congress towards the end of April 2005.[30] Caveat emptor!

Governmental Resistance to Regulating Biowarfare Research

Not surprisingly, the Reagan administration fought our CRG draft legislation tooth and claw. The Reaganites knew full well that our legislation was designed to stop what they were doing at the Pentagon, in U.S. government labs, and at American universities by means of the BDRP. In the draft legislation I made it crystal clear that the research, development, and testing of such biowarfare agents would be punished by life in prison. I do not believe in the death penalty for any reason, so I did not put that ultimate penalty into the legislation. But I did intend to scare the living daylights out of any life-science researcher contemplating getting involved with a dual-use, simultaneously offensive-defensive biowarfare DNA genetic engineering project for the Pentagon, CIA, and the Department of Agriculture (DOA), which was also contemporaneously pouring large amounts of money into the research, development and testing of offensive biowarfare agents against plants and animals in violation of BWC article I. Today the "Department of Homeland Security" is also doing the exact same thing under the Bush Jr. administration.[31] In fact, this gratuitously needless proliferation of dual-use, simultaneously offensive-defensive biowarfare technology shall create massive insecurity for the American people.

The Neo-Cons under Reagan
Violate the Biological Weapons Convention

What we did not know at the time that the Reaganite Neo-Cons were fighting us tooth and claw over the CRG draft legislation was that they had already authorized multiple shipments of weapons-specific biological agents to Iraq from the American Type Culture Collection (ATCC) and the U.S. Centers for Disease Control and Prevention (CDC) in the hope and expectation that Saddam Hussein would weaponize these biowarfare agents and then use them against Iran during the course of the on-going Iraq-Iran War. ATCC is a large private-sector scientific institute that cultures and stores every known type of disease occurring in nature for supposedly scientific purposes. It is therefore striking to note that both ATCC and CDC went along with the Reagan administration's wanton breach of the BWC by shipping these weapons-specific bio-agents to Iraq.[32] While the ATCC might be induced to jeopardize its reputation because of governmental pressure, what is one to say of the CDC, whose mandate and very name commits it to work on behalf of disease *control* and *prevention*!

The Reaganite Neo-Cons' transshipments of these weapons-specific biological agents to Saddam Hussein clearly violated BWC article III:

> Each State Party to this Convention undertakes not to transfer to any recipient whatsoever, directly or indirectly, and not in any way to assist, encourage, or induce any State, group of States or international organizations to manufacture or otherwise acquire any of the agents, toxins, weapons, equipment or means of delivery specified in article I of the Convention.

Under the proposed CRG draft implementing legislation these biowarfare transshipments to Iraq would have subjected these Reaganite perpetrators to life in prison, so they fought the CRG draft implementing legislation right up to the time of their (temporary) political demise, which occurred when Bush Sr. was elected President in November of 1988.

The Bush Sr. Administration
Acts Responsibly on Biowarfare

With the advent of the Bush Sr. administration to power, President George H.W. Bush and his Secretary of State, Jim Baker, proceeded to clean house by getting rid of many of the Reaganite Neo-Cons, and replacing them with foreign affairs and defense experts drawn from the traditional wing of the Republican Party Establishment going back to the Nixon administration, which had originally supported the BWC. To the great and everlasting credit of the Bush Sr. administration, shortly after they came into power in January of 1989 and got organized, all opposition to our CRG draft legislation by the Executive Branch of the United States government suddenly disappeared. Miraculously, the CRG draft legislation was put on the Congressional fast-track for presidential signing into law. Mirabile dictu!

Meanwhile, the CRG was advised that it would help our lobbying efforts on Capitol Hill if we could repackage, reposition, and represent our legislation to Congress as a new law designed to deal with biological warfare agents developed by terrorists somewhere in the Third World who could threaten the United States of America. We, on the other hand, were primarily concerned about the biowarfare-related activities of the Neo-Cons in the Pentagon and the complicity of private-sector death-scientists working for them at American universities and in U.S. government labs pursuant to the BDRP. But we felt if that was the public relations approach we needed to adopt in order to get this legislation passed through Congress, then so be it! We did not alter the basic thrust of the legislative text one iota. We simply repackaged the CRG draft law as legislation designed to counteract bioterrorism against the United States by "crazies" out there in the Third World.[33] But it was the "crazies" lurking in the Reaganite

Neo-Con Pentagon and their atrocious BDRP death-scientist accomplices at American universities and in U.S. government labs with whom we were almost exclusively concerned.

As a result of this public relations repackaging, the CRG legislation was adopted unanimously by both Houses of Congress, and signed into law by President Bush Sr. on 22 May 1990 under the official title of the "Biological Weapons Anti-Terrorism Act of 1989"[34] (hereinafter referred to as the Act).

To their great credit, the Bush Sr. administration slowed down the BDRP[35] and terminated the Reaganites' biowarfare shipments to Saddam Hussein in Iraq.[36] Since then, in direct reaction to subsequent events during the past fifteen years that I will not bother to review here, the original CRG Act has been repeatedly revised and is now presently codified into United States Code, Title 18 Crimes and Criminal Procedure, Part I. Crimes, Chapter 10, Biological Weapons, Sections 175 to 178 (as of 8 September 2004).

Primary Features of the Biological Weapons Anti-Terrorism Act

I will not go through the legislative history of the Act here, nor perform a detailed analysis of this Act as currently amended. But for the purposes of this study, its most salient features are as follows:

> § 175. Prohibitions with respect to biological weapons.[37]
>
> (a) In general. Whoever knowingly develops, produces, stockpiles, transfers, acquires, retains, or possesses any biological agent, toxin, or delivery system for use as a weapon, or knowingly assists a foreign state or any organization to do so, or attempts, threatens, or conspires to do the same, shall be fined under this title or imprisoned for life or any

term of years, or both. There is extraterritorial Federal jurisdiction over an offense under this section committed by or against a national of the United States.

(b) Additional offense. Whoever knowingly possesses any biological agent, toxin, or delivery system of a type or in a quantity that, under the circumstances, is not reasonably justified by a prophylactic, protective, bona fide research, or other peaceful purpose, shall be fined under this title, imprisoned not more than 10 years, or both. In this subsection, the terms "biological agent" and "toxin" do not encompass any biological agent or toxin that is in its naturally occurring environment, if the biological agent or toxin has not been cultivated, collected, or otherwise extracted from its natural source.

(c) Definition. For purposes of this section, the term "for use as a weapon" includes the development, production, transfer, acquisition, retention, or possession of any biological agent, toxin, or delivery system for other than prophylactic, protective, bona fide research, or other peaceful purposes.

. . . .

§ 178. Definitions[38]

As used in this chapter:

> **(1)** the term "biological agent" means any microorganism (including, but not limited to, bacterial, viruses, fungi, rickettsiae or protozoa), or infectious

substance, or any naturally occurring, bioengineered or synthesized component of any such microorganism or infectious substance, capable of causing

(A) death, disease, or other biological malfunction in a human, an animal, a plant, or another living organism;

(B) deterioration of food, water, equipment, supplies, or material of any kind; or

(C) deleterious alteration of the environment;

(2) the term "toxin" means the toxic material or product of plants, animals, microorganisms (including, but not limited to, bacteria, viruses, fungi, rickettsiae or protozoa), or infectious substances, or a recombinant or synthesized molecule, whatever their origin and method of production, and includes

(A) any poisonous substance or biological product that may be engineered as a result of biotechnology produced by a living organism; or

(B) any poisonous isomer or biological product, homolog, or derivative of such a substance;

(3) the term "delivery system" means

(A) any apparatus, equipment, device, or means of delivery specifically designed to deliver or disseminate a biological agent, toxin, or vector; or

(B) any vector;

(4) the term "vector" means a living organism, or molecule, including a recombinant or synthesized molecule, capable of carrying a biological agent or toxin to a host; and

(5) the term "national of the United States" has the meaning prescribed in section 101(a)(22) of the Immigration and Nationality Act (8 U.S.C. 1101(a)(22)).

Closing the Door on Biowarfare Research Loopholes

The Biological Weapons Anti-Terrorism Act of 1989 as currently amended in the United States Code closes any loopholes and fills in any lacunae that even conceivably might arguably have been found in the text of the BWC itself. Now, as far as the United States of America is concerned, the BWC must be interpreted and applied by reference to this Act as currently revised for the purposes of both international law and U.S. domestic law. The present Act sets forth the U.S. government's own official interpretation of its treaty obligations under the BWC that is legally binding upon it and all U.S. nationals and residents under both public international law as well as U.S. domestic criminal law.

Likewise, foreign governments must evaluate U.S. compliance with the BWC by reference to both the BWC text and its CRG domestic implementing legislation as currently amended. Foreign states parties to the BWC must demand that the United States government obey the BWC in strict accordance with the text of the treaty itself as well as domestically implemented by the present Act. When conjoined with the BWC, the current Act becomes an extremely powerful and comprehensive package of combined international and domestic law that both American civil society and the international community can and must bring to bear upon the United States government itself as well as upon U.S. private-sector death-scientists in order to stop their dual-use, simultaneously offensive-defensive DNA genetic engineering projects for biowarfare purposes.

CHAPTER FIVE

U.S. BIOWARFARE- RELATED VIOLATIONS OF INTERNATIONAL LAW

Iraq: The Nuremberg Code on Medical Experimentation

Let us return the analysis to the weapons-specific biological agents shipped to Saddam Hussein by the American Type Culture Collection and the U.S. Centers for Disease Control and Prevention at the behest of the Reagan administration and its Neo-Cons, many of whom now inhabit the Bush Jr. administration, who, as above-mentioned, had already violated the terms of the Biological Weapons Convention.

In the late fall of 1990, as the Bush Sr. administration raced to war against Iraq,[39] the then Secretary of "Defense" Richard Cheney (now Bush Jr.'s Vice President and in the eyes of many, the de facto President of the United States of America) ordered all U.S. armed forces deploying for the zone of hostilities to be inoculated with experimental medical vaccines for anthrax and botulin toxin not only prior to vaccine approval by the F.D.A., but without their informed consent and thereby in clear cut violation of the Nuremberg Code on Medical Experimentation.[40]

At the time we had no idea why the vaccines were so necessary. The reason became quite clear later on, when it was learned that the Reagan administration had surreptitiously shipped these weapons-specific biological agents to Iraq, and it was felt that Saddam Hussein had weaponized the anthrax and botulin toxin. The Bush Sr. administration knew full well that U.S. armed forces attacking Iraq would be vulnerable to these biowarfare agents that the Reaganite Neo-Cons had provided to Saddam Hussein for the express purpose of weaponization and use against Iran. "Blowback" indeed.

As always, the first illegal misstep compelled the second, which was criminal. Accordingly, what were then only experimental medical vaccines were injected into the 500,000 U.S. armed forces deployed for Gulf War I by the Bush Sr. administration, as well as into the British troops similarly designated, turning the entire project into a massive live experiment, the results of which—due to its irregularity and indeed illegality—neither the scientific research community nor the Pentagon were able to counteract, since records of the effects of the vaccines were systematically NOT kept— whether to prevent public or soldier knowledge and reconstruction of the experimental nature of the vaccines being forcibly administered, or indeed, to subsequently prohibit the collation of negative findings to be used against the responsible Bush Sr. administration officials.

As of today, more than 11,000 U.S. troops have died— but not from combat—and most of the rest suffer from the Gulf War Syndrome (GWS). Of course, depleted uranium (DU) munitions were and remain another causative factor behind GWS.[41] The Pentagon continues to deny that there is such a medical phenomenon categorized as Gulf War Syndrome— even beyond the point where everyone knows that denial is pure propaganda and disinformation. The Pentagon will never own up to the legal, economic, tortious, political, and criminal consequences of admitting the existence of GWS. So U.S.

and U.K. veterans of Gulf War I as well as their afterborn children will continue to suffer and die. The same will prove true for U.S. and U.K. veterans of Bush Jr.'s Gulf War II as well as their afterborn children.

Bush Sr., Cheney, General Colin Powell (then Chairman of the Joint Chiefs of Staff and later Bush Jr.'s first Secretary of State), General "Stormin'" Norman Schwarzkopf, and the rest of the U.S. military High Command inflicted a Nuremberg Crime on United States armed forces by forcing them to take these experimental medical vaccines in violation of the Nuremberg Code on Medical Experimentation. I first argued this point in the 1991 U.S. Army court-martial proceedings against Captain Doctor Yolanda Huet-Vaughn, who was persecuted in part for refusing to give these experimental medical vaccines to U.S. armed forces then deploying for Bush Sr.'s Gulf War I.[42] Later Senator Jay Rockefeller conducted public hearings on this scandal, at the conclusion of which he also accused senior members of the Bush Sr. administration of perpetrating a Nuremberg Crime on America's own troops.[43]

The Clinton Administration
Violates the Biological Weapons Convention

As card-carrying members of America's power elite, Democrats too have engaged in internationally criminal acts. The Clinton administration's self-styled Neo-Liberals decided to reactivate massive Pentagon funding for dual-use, simultaneously offensive-defensive DNA genetic engineering biowarfare contracts despite the fact that the Reaganite Neo-Cons and their BDRP scientist accomplices had already "researched" most naturally occurring bio-agents to death almost a decade beforehand.

Then the *New York Times* broke the story:[44]

> • A U.S. government agency was developing an immune resistant strain of anthrax by means of DNA genetic engineering.

• A U.S. government agency had developed super-weapons grade anthrax in quantities and strengths that had no legitimate "defensive" purpose whatsoever.

• A U.S. government agency had constructed a biowarfare bomb factory where they were testing their capability to "produce" biological weapons.

Other government contracts let out by the Clintonite Neo-Liberal Pentagon to U.S. private-sector death-scientists called for the aerosolization of DNA genetically engineered bio-agents—an obvious, though not necessarily conclusive, tip-off for an illegal, offensive and criminal biowarfare program. Aerosolization is critical to the weaponization of bio-agents because most are delivered to human beings by air.[45]

These Clintonite Neo-Liberal biowarfare programs violated both the Biological Weapons Convention, and the Biological Weapons Anti-Terrorism Act of 1989, initiated by the Committee for Responsible Genetics.

The George W. Bush Administration
Repudiates the Verification Protocol of the BWC

It came as no surprise that at the first available opportunity in July of 2001, the new Bush Jr. administration and its recycled Reaganite Neo-Cons repudiated the Verification Protocol for the Biological Weapons Convention that had been under international negotiation for quite some time.[46] The watering-down, stalling, and degradation of the BWC Verification Protocol by the Neo-Lib Clinton administration[47] that was followed almost immediately by its outright repudiation by the Neo-Con Bush Jr. administration clearly violated the preambular language of the BWC mandating effective measures to eliminate all weapons of mass destruction (nuclear, biological, and chemical) in general, and biowarfare agents in particular:

The States Parties to this Convention,

Determined to act with a view to achieving effective progress towards general and complete disarmament, including the prohibition and elimination of all types of weapons of mass destruction, and convinced that the prohibition of the development, production and stockpiling of chemical and bacteriological (biological) weapons and their elimination, through effective measures, will facilitate the achievement of general and complete disarmament under strict and effective international control.

. . . .

Convinced of the importance and urgency of eliminating from the arsenals of States, through effective measures, such dangerous weapons of mass destruction as those using chemical or bacteriological (biological) agents.

. . . . .

Since both the Republican Neo-Cons and the Democrat Neo-Liberals agreed with the Machiavellian principle that "the best defense is a good offense" when it came to the research, development, and testing of biological weapons, the American power elite was united in the conviction that it would be counterproductive to have a strict and effective international monitoring and inspection mechanism for the Biological Weapons Convention—which would be unverifiable without it. Indeed, there was no reason for the wolf to appoint a shepherd to guard the sheep when the wolf planned to eat the sheep. Bush Jr. was already preparing to set loose the dogs of war on Afghanistan, Iraq, and elsewhere. That is also why, from the very moment of its inception, the Bush Jr. administration has done everything humanly possible to sabotage the International Criminal Court.[48]

All evidence of consciousness of guilt. All the likeliest sign of it.

CHAPTER SIX

DOMESTIC TERRORISM: THE ANTHRAX ATTACKS ON THE U.S. CONGRESS

The history of U.S. biowarfare research took on a major twist right after 11 September 2001 with the terrorist anthrax attacks upon the United States Congress. Originally it was not clear to me what was going on—not until the *New York Times* published the biotechnology behind the Daschle Letter.

The anthrax in the Daschle letter was extremely sophis-ticated: super-weapons-grade anthrax with a special treatment designed to eliminate electrostatic charges so it could float in the air.[49] The only scientists who would have had the capability to manufacture this would be individuals who either are currently employed, or had been employed, by the U.S. government's biowarfare program. Arguably, they were currently employed, since they would have had to have had access to one of the U.S. government's high-containment biowarfare labs in order to process and assemble these bioterrorism weapons; and would probably have to have worn one of their so-called "moonsuits" in order to do so in safety. Those precise criteria narrowed the list of potential culprits down to a manageable handful.

Immediately after reading the article in the *New York Times*, I placed two phone calls to Marion "Spike" Bowman—to whom I will return below—a senior official in the FBI who handles terrorism and counter-terrorism and knew of the work I had done in the field of biowarfare in order to discuss this matter with him. I told him that there are very few people who had this technological capability and physical access to the required facilities, and that I could save him some steps by providing a list of these individuals under the Reaganite Biological Defense Research Program (BDRP). I then went down the list of names and labs of U.S. "life-scientists" who had worked on anthrax for the Reaganite BDRP. I also told him that he could get the current lists of U.S. "life-scientists" now working on anthrax at the Pentagon and the CIA since the Clinton administration had vamped up the U.S. government's biowarfare program.

He responded by saying that the FBI was coordinating its investigation with Fort Detrick.

I bluntly told him that Fort Detrick could very well be the problem here: that this could be a Timothy McVeigh-type situation where someone who was once on the reservation is now off the reservation. I made it clear that the FBI could not trust the people at Fort Detrick.

He told me that he would pass my information along to the FBI personnel handling the anthrax investigation. My suspicion about Fort Detrick being the source of the biological agent behind these terrorist anthrax attacks was later confirmed.

This conversation transpired just before I conducted a Workshop on Biowarfare on behalf of the Council for Responsible Genetics at Harvard Divinity School on Saturday, 3 November 2001. There my CRG colleague and co-panelist, Jonathan King, Professor of Microbiology at MIT and the Director of their Electron-Microscope Lab, publicly stated that he had reached the exact same conclusion independently: Someone working for the U.S. government's biowarfare program must have been behind these terrorist anthrax attacks.

That same day on the front steps of Harvard Divinity School I was interviewed by Fox TV News for Boston and expressed the same opinion. And a few days later I was interviewed on

BBC World Service and also on Pacifica Radio Network News in Washington D.C. as well as by the *Albuquerque Journal* in New Mexico to the same effect. Likewise, my former CRG colleague, Dr. Barbara Rosenberg, who was then handling biowarfare for the Federation of American Scientists, independently of both Professor King and myself, later stated the exact same conclusion in public: that whoever perpetrated this act of bioterrorism had been working for a United States government biowarfare program, and must have had access to a U.S. biowarfare lab, and have worn a "moonsuit."[50]

It had been an act of *domestic* terrorism—committed by persons who, at the very least, were once working for the government, and arguably were working for it still! Exactly what I had sought to prevent two decades ago when I had publicly proposed enacting U.S. domestic implementing legislation for the BWC on 13 September 1985 on Congress' Capitol Hill in Washington D.C., now the victim of these terrorist anthrax attacks sixteen years later. It was not those "crazies" somewhere out there in the Third World who had launched a terrorist attack on the oldest republican deliberative body in the world. Rather, it was domestic terrorists—the "crazies" in the Pentagon, or the CIA, or their death-scientist accomplices in the U.S. private-sector—who had attacked, terrorized and shut down the United States Congress in an action which seems plausible to regard as linked to the other terrorist attacks that immediately preceded them on 11 September 2001.

The FBI Cover-Up: Motivating Factors

Despite my explicit informational warning to the FBI, soon thereafter the FBI authorized the destruction of the U.S. government's anthrax culture collection at Ames, Iowa[51]—despite the fact that it had been determined that the substance used in the terrorist anthrax attacks on the U.S. Congress was Ames-strain anthrax coming from the U.S. government biowarfare lab at Fort Detrick.[52] At the very least, this appears to be a cover-up orchestrated by the FBI. Does it seem implausible to think that this is being done at the behest of its Bush Jr. Neo-Con superiors?

If independent life-scientists at the CRG had had access to the Ames Anthrax collection, they could have performed genetic reconstructions of the Daschle Letter and the Leahy Letter in order to pin-point precisely where, when, and from whom these bio-agents had originated. The trail of genetic evidence would have led directly back to a secret but officially-sponsored U.S. government biowarfare program that was illegal and criminal, in violation of the Biological Weapons Convention and the revised Biological Weapons Anti-Terrorism Act of 1989 (the CRG Act) that had been undertaken by the Pentagon, or the CIA, or their U.S. private-sector death-scientist accomplices, or all acting in conjunction with each other.

I believe the FBI knows exactly who was behind these terrorist anthrax attacks upon the United States Congress in the Fall of 2001, and that the culprits were U.S. government-related scientists involved in a criminal U.S. government biowarfare program that violated both the BWC and U.S. domestic legislation implementing the same.[53] For that reason, the FBI is not going to apprehend and have indicted the culprits because the ensuing legal process would, in a court of law, directly implicate the United States government itself, its agencies, its officials, and its agents, in conducting illegal and criminal biowarfare research, development, testing, and use in violation of the Biological Weapons Convention and the revised Biological Weapons Anti-Terrorism Act, which, as domestic implementing legislation, requires U.S. domestic prosecution on such charges.

While in many instances, U.S. adherence to international treaties is framed in such a manner as to inhibit American citizens from being able to address U.S. violations in American courts, the 1989 implementing legislation for the BWC has enabled this option. Were the perpetrator to be brought to trial, the extensive legal processes involved in determination of criminal guilt would of necessity direct public attention to current U.S. biowarfare research and development, and the dangers and illegalities thereof. Down the road, it could give rise to a host of lawsuits by outraged American institutions, NGOs, and individuals contending current or past biological research and development programs contravene or have contravened both the BWC and the 1989 domestic BWC implementing legislation as amended, and seeking to force exposure of past or present programs for examination for possible criminal prosecutions and civil lawsuits for damages.

Once under the glare of a domestic and international public spotlight, the ramifications could stream off in all directions: further damage to U.S. international credibility, a threat to the standing of the Biological Weapons Convention, the initiation of a global "defensive" bioweapons arms race, the review of related biowarfare issues as they concern American citizens— the forced administration of both the anthrax vaccine to American military personnel and the smallpox vaccine to American public health workers, the safety and public welfare of these programs—thereby jeopardizing billions of dollars dedicated to biowarfare "defense," etc.

Resounding Silence

As part of this ongoing cover-up, the FBI went out and retained every independent life-scientist it could locate as part of its fictitious investigation, and then swore them all to secrecy so that they cannot publicly comment on the investigation or give their expert opinion to the American people about who really was behind these terrorist anthrax attacks upon the American Congress.[54] This may be why there is nothing but an FBI-imposed "deafening silence" coming from the U.S. life-scientist community on the terrorist anthrax attacks—except for a few courageous and independently-minded individuals such as Professor King of M.I.T. and Dr. Rosenberg of the Federation of American Scientists. While it is to be expected that the FBI will eventually proceed to finger a *private-sector* death-scientist for these crimes, in all likelihood this will be done only to make it appear that they have actually been conducting a productive investigation, and to shut down any further enquiry.

Or the FBI could spin out their bogus investigation forever, while most of America's life-scientists are pledged to secrecy, genuinely believing in good faith that they are helping the FBI track down the culprits. Meanwhile, the FBI tosses out the names of some—again, private-sector—U.S. death-scientists as red meat to the news media for public relations consumption as potential suspects:[55] He who supps with the devil had better bring a long spoon.

And what about Congress? It was, after all, a target of domestic bio-terrorism. Its members were swept from the congressional halls. Some, indeed, might even have been killed. And yet to date the U.S. Congress has not opened an official investigation into this terrorist attack upon it. Perhaps the Members of Congress fear that they could become the next targets of a new round of terrorist anthrax attacks along the lines of Senators Daschle and Leahy? Perhaps the Members of Congress are not convinced by the suspicious public explanation for the tragic death of the crusading Senator Paul Wellstone?

As for the corporate-controlled public news media, one wonders if it even remembers that the event remains unsolved.

Linkage Between the Anthrax Attacks and 9/11?

By means of this little charade, the greatest *political* crime in the history of the United States of America since its founding on 4 July 1776—the anthrax attacks on Congress, which served not only to deliver a terrorist threat to its members, but actually to close it down for a period—may remain officially unresolved forever. Could it truly be coincidental that two of the primary intended victims of the terrorist anthrax attacks—Senators Daschle and Leahy—were holding up the speedy passage of the pre-planned USA Patriot Act after the terrible tragedy of 11 September 2001—an Act which provided the federal government with unprecedented powers in relation to US citizens and institutions?[56]

This analysis ultimately begs the broader question: Who really was behind the terrorist attacks of 11 September 2001?

A substantial body of reputable opinion now argues that it was agents affiliated with the clandestine services of the United States government who were ultimately behind the terrorist attacks of 11 September 2001.[57] Even the distinguished International Law Professor Richard Falk has supported this line of inquiry.[58] Could it be that what really happened in the fall of 2001 was the proverbial "one-two punch" against the American Republic and the U.S. Constitution by the Pentagon, the CIA, the National Security Council, the FBI and the rest of what the former Soviet Union used to call its "power ministries": NSA, DIA, NRO, etc. In other words, could America have suffered—without even remarking it—a coup d'état? Could it be that Americans are today living under a military dictatorship *cum* police state that we are only now gradually beginning to figure out, deal with, and struggle against?

In this regard, let me return the analysis to the significant role played by the previously mentioned FBI Agent, Marion "Spike" Bowman in failing to prevent the terrorist attacks on 11 September 2001. In particular it has been reported that Mr. Bowman played the pivotal role by suppressing evidence which in turn prevented the issuance of a search warrant for the computer of Zacarias Moussaoui, the alleged 20th al-Qaeda hijacker on 11 September 2001, which might otherwise have led to foreknowledge and therefore prevention of those terrorist attacks in the first place:[59]

> . . . The Minneapolis [F.B.I.] request [for the search warrant] was then given to RFU [Radical Fundamentalist Unit] agent Marion "Spike" Bowman, who lived up to his nickname by proceeding to remove the evidence that Moussaoui was connected to al-Qaeda through a rebel group in Chechnya. Then the FBI Deputy General Counsel, on the basis of this edited request, said that there was insufficient connection to al-Qaeda for a search warrant and did not even forward the request to FISA. Minneapolis FBI legal officer Coleen

> Rowley asked: "Why would an FBI agent deliberately sabotage a case?" Other agents in the Minneapolis office joked that those at headquarters who blocked the request "had to be spies or moles. . . working for Osama bin Laden," while one agent concluded that FBI headquarters was "setting this up for failure."
>
> . . . .
>
> For example, Marion "Spike" Bowman—the agent at FBI headquarters who altered the Minneapolis FBI's request for the warrant to search Moussaoui's belongings—was in December of 2002 given an FBI award for "exceptional performance." This award came, furthermore, after a congressional report said that Bowman's RFU unit had given Minneapolis FBI agents "inexcusably confused and inaccurate information" that was "patently fake."

Could it be that F.B.I. Agent Bowman received an F.B.I. award for "exceptional performance" because of his capacity, demonstrated in both instances mentioned above, to *forestall* investigations, because of where they may lead? Could the real culprits behind the terrorist attacks on 11 September 2001 and the immediately following terrorist anthrax attacks upon Congress ultimately prove to be the same people?

As we go to press, these news items seem noteworthy:

• Douglas Jehl, writing in the *New York Times* on August 9th, confirms what has been widely reported overseas but long covered up by the Bush administration and the American media: Mohammed Atta, believed to be the operational leader of the 9/11 attacks, was under US intelligence surveillance even before he came to the United States in 2000. The military team "recommended to the military's Special Operations Command that the information be shared with the Federal Bureau of Investigation . . . The recommendation was rejected and the information was not shared . . ." What this means is that over a two year period, Atta (along with, in later accounts, three other members of Al-Qaeda) entered and re-entered the United States as they undertook the many activities necessary for their preparation for an attack on the World Trade Center—including learning how to fly the planes—all with the Pentagon being fully aware of, permitting, and at no point intercepting or preventing, their activities.[60]

• According to a report published on August 8th by the *Washington Post*, the Pentagon has developed its first ever plans for operations within the continental United States related to the imposition of martial law on cities, regions or the entire country—irrespective of a long-standing congressional prohibition on the use of the military for domestic policing, known as the Posse Comitatus Act. The plans are extensive, despite the fact that no further terrorist attacks have occurred within the US since 9/11. "The possible scenarios range from 'low end,' relatively modest crowd-control missions to 'high-end,' full-scale disaster management, after catastrophic attacks such as the release of a deadly biological agent or the explosion of a radiological device...."[61]

CHAPTER SEVEN

GEARING UP TO FIGHT AND "WIN" BIOWARFARE

Today the United States government is spending more money in constant, inflation-adjusted dollars on biowarfare research and development than it did a generation ago on the Manhattan Project for the research and development of the atom bomb during World War II, [62] which was then utilized to criminally obliterate the civilian populations of Hiroshima and Nagasaki, and establish American dominance in the Pacific Rim for over half a century. [63]

The amounts of money being poured into ramping up the U.S. biowarfare industry are truly staggering. [64] For fiscal years 2001 through 2004, the United States government has funded a sum total of $14.5 billion dollars for ostensibly "civilian" biowarfare-related work alone, with an additional $7.6 billion requested for fiscal year 2005. This "civilian" biowarfare poisoned pork has been carved up among the Department of Health and Human Services (68%), Department of Homeland Security (22%), Department of Defense (5%), Department of Agriculture (3%), Environmental Protection Agency (2%), National Science Foundation (under 1%), and the Department of State (under 1%).

The deceptively-named "Project BioShield" alone has been funded to the tune of $5.6 billion for the next decade. [65] Under the auspices of the Department of Homeland Security, Project BioSheild authorizes the expenditure of $5.6 billion over ten years for the federal government supposedly "to purchase and stockpile vaccines and drugs to fight anthrax, smallpox and other potential agents of bioterror."[66]   The terrorist attacks of 11 September 2001 and the terrorist anthrax attacks upon the U.S. Congress have been cited by President Bush—and commonly accepted by the American public—as the justification for his signing the BioShield Act of 2004.   But the anthrax attacks, at least, may prove to more properly be seen as a pretext for the launching of a major new program devoted to addressing one of the fundamental requirements for effectively waging biowarfare: protection of the civilian population.

On top of those figures for "civilian" biowarfare work must also be added the Pentagon's overt chemical and biological warfare program in the amount of $2.34 billion for fiscal years 2001—2004, with $560 million requested for FY 2005.

WMD Partnering: Nuclear and Bioweaponry

The above mind-boggling figures do not even include the national nuclear weapons laboratories for the Department of Energy that are also hopping on the gravy train for biowarfare research and development,[67] under the highly contestable premise that such biowarfare work neatly complements their research, development, and testing of nuclear weapons. Any objective analyst must conclude that for U.S. nuclear weapons labs to get involved in biowarfare work raises a prima facie and grievous non-compliance problem with the BWC.

It is highly doubtful that foreign states will accept DoE labs' self-interested public assurances that insofar as they have been involved in the research, development, testing, and use of offensive nuclear weapons since the Manhattan Project, they should be trusted to *refrain* from getting involved in the research, development, testing, and offensive use of biological weapons. After a generation of continuous research, development, testing and use of weapons of mass destruction (WMD) going back to the mass exterminations at Hiroshima and Nagasaki, it would strain anyone's sense of the credible to suppose that now, all of a sudden, these nuclear weapons labs' true mission will be to perform scientific research with respect to biological weapons for the benefit of humanity even as they simultaneously continue to pursue apace their development of the next generation of offensive nuclear weapons of mass destruction. After all, shortly after the Fall 2001 terrorist attacks of September 11 and the anthrax attacks on the U.S. Congress, the Bush Jr. administration's Neo-conservative Deputy Secretary of Defense, Paul Wolfowitz, publicly admitted that despite long-standing U.S. governmental assurances to the contrary, the U.S. strategic nuclear "deterrent" had always consisted of "an almost exclusive emphasis on *offensive* nuclear forces."[68]   Is there a good reason for the world to believe similar U.S. government propaganda concerning the "defensive" purposes of the Pentagon's self-styled Chemical and Biological Defense Program (CBDP) that was developed directly under Wolfowitz's watch at the Pentagon?

PNAC Bombshell a Harbinger?

The Reaganite Neo-conservative Project for a New American Century(PNAC), whose members heavily influenced the formulation and execution of   the Bush Jr. administration's foreign affairs and "defense" policies and staffed its bureaucracies, in their seminal report on Rebuilding America's Defenses (September 2000) publicly recommended numerous policies for adoption by the United States government. In particular:

> And advanced forms of biological warfare that can 'target' specific genotypes may transform biological warfare from the realm of terror to a politically useful tool.

And also:

> Munitions themselves will becoming increasingly accurate, while new methods of attack—electronic, 'non-lethal', biological— will be more widely available.

Then PNACer Paul Wolfowitz signed on to this report. For reasons that will become clear below, Wolfowitz and his fellow PNACers soon entered the new Bush Jr. administration starting in early 2001 and proceeded to implement the PNAC Report, including its call for the development of biological weapons.

The Bush Jr. Administration's Plans for Bio-WMD Wars of Aggression[69]

In September 2002, under the direct influence of Neo-Cons such as Wolfowitz, the Bush Jr. administration officially approved and adopted the "National Security Strategy of the United States" that articulated the doctrine of preventive warfare—that the U.S. would not limit itself to waging war in self-defense, but rather would take first-strike action against countries which it professed might have the intent and means to attack the U.S.—and transmitted it to the United States Congress as a declaration of official policy by the United States of America. Then, while it was publicly campaigning for a war of aggression against Iraq pursuant to this national strategy directive, in December 2002, the Bush Jr. administration released its even more disturbing "National Strategy to Combat Weapons of Mass Destruction." This supplementary war plan calls for the first use of weapons of mass destruction (WMD)—"including through resort to all of our options"–by the United States government under the justification of waging preventive or preemptive warfare that had been promulgated in the September 2002 national strategy directive. As elaborated more fully in my book, *Destroying World Order* (2004),[70] these Neo-Con Bush Jr. doctrines of preventive warfare are nothing more than pretexts for waging illegal wars of aggression, as exemplified by the aggressive, illegal, and criminal war against Iraq launched by the United States in March of 2003.

It is important to underline that in December 2002, the Bush Jr. administration officially announced that the United States was fully prepared to be the first state to use WMD for aggressive purposes. It would do so against its chosen adversaries around the world as part of an offensive military operation, or even to launch a full-scale war itself. Notice, therefore, that since December 2002, the United States government has had in place an official policy providing the policy framework it would need in order to initiate, fight and "win" a war of aggression by means of nuclear, biological, and chemical (NBC) weapons of mass destruction (WMD). What public debate in the U.S. Congress or elsewhere has there been on this implementation of official preparedness to exercise what is an astounding acceleration in aggressive intent and possible action in American foreign policy: U.S. preparedness to wage a first-strike bioweaponry war?

These Bush Jr. national security directives of September 2002 and December 2002 unconstitutionally usurp and nullify the right and the power of the United States Congress to declare war in gross and blatant violation of Article I, Section 8, Clause 11 of the United States Constitution. They constitute the final and terminal culmination of the process of consolidating an imperial presidency described by Professor Arthur M. Schlesinger Jr. in his classic 1973 study.[71]

The illegality of such doctrines of preventive warfare was entrenched by the Nuremberg Tribunal, which rejected the Nazi defendants' attempt to make this reprehensible argument in order to justify their invasion of Norway. In explicitly endorsing the well-known *Caroline Case* (1837), the Nuremberg Tribunal enshrined this test as a basic principle of the post-World War II international legal order: "It must be remembered that preventive action in foreign territory is justified only in case of 'an instant and overwhelming necessity for self-defense, leaving no choice of means, and no moment of deliberation' (The *Caroline Case*)."

Moreover, in order to further justify their preventive war against Norway, the Nazi defendants had argued that in accordance with German reservations on self-defense made at the time of the conclusion of the Kellogg-Briand Peace Pact of 1928, Germany alone could decide whether preventive action was necessary, and also that in making such a decision, Germany's judgment was conclusive. In rejecting this Nazi self-judging argument, the Nuremberg Tribunal emphatically ruled: "But whether action taken under the claim of self-defense was in fact aggressive or defensive must ultimately be subject to investigation and adjudication if international law is ever to be enforced." Notwithstanding this seminal jurisprudence, today the Bush Jr. administration is planning, preparing and conspiring to wage aggressive warfare by means of NBC/WMD whose destructive powers far exceed even the wildest fantasies of Hitler and the Nazis in blatant violation of the Nuremberg Charter, the Nuremberg Judgment, and the Nuremberg Principles.

Bush Undersecretary of State for Arms Control— Gung Ho for Bios

At the start of his second term in office, President Bush Jr. appointed the Neo-Conservative operative Robert Joseph to serve as his new Undersecretary of State for Arms Control and International Security Affairs, replacing the ultra-hawkish Neo-Con, John Bolton. Previously Joseph had worked at the Bush Jr. White House National Security Council, where he had formulated and implemented the aforementioned September 2002 National Security Strategy directive, the December 2002 National Strategy to Combat Weapons of Mass Destruction, the National Strategy for Biodefense, and the withdrawal from the 1972 Anti-Ballistic Missile Systems Treaty in 2001. Quite a litany of criminality, recklessness, deceit, and obfuscation that will not be fully addressed here. But for the purposes of this book, Joseph is on record for being against arms control for biological weapons: "At worst, as we discovered in the draft BWC Protocol that we inherited, an arms control approach would actually harm our ability to deal with the WMD threat."[72] In other words, the current Undersecretary of State for Arms Control is openly against arms control for biological weapons. Truly Orwellian. Yet another example of President Bush Jr. putting a fox in charge of a henhouse.

To Fight and "Win" by Biowarfare: The Prerequisites

During the Reagan administration, the Neo-Cons at the Pentagon adopted a policy and implemented programs to the effect that the United States government would prepare to fight and "win" a nuclear war.[73] Now some of these same Neo-Cons during the Bush Jr. administration such as Wolfowitz have adopted the policy and are implementing programs to the effect that the United States government must prepare to fight offensively and "win" through waging biological warfare. In theory, this offensive strategy for launching biological warfare requires two elemental programmatic components:

> 1. The Pentagon must develop and produce an arsenal of proven biowarfare agents together with effective delivery systems and dispersal mechanisms.

> 2. The United States government must prepare adequate biowarfare "defenses" in order to protect America's civilian population at home from anticipated biowarfare retaliation by an adversary as well as from "blowback" upon invading U.S. troops and on the American "homeland" resulting from the Pentagon overtly or the CIA covertly unleashing biological warfare pursuant to the aforementioned Bush Jr. September 2002 and December 2002 national strategy directives— or from any catastrophic accidental release of biological warfare agents which might occur during research and production of same.

The Smoking Gun: The Pentagon's Chemical and Biological Defense Program

The first component necessary for the Neo-Con Bush Jr. administration to fight and "win" using biological warfare is a program to research, test, and develop effective and proven biowarfare agents. This has now been set forth by the Pentagon in its Final Programmatic Environmental Impact Statement (FPEIS) for its self-styled Chemical and Biological Defense

Program (CBDP) that was published in May of 2004. This FPEIS/CBDP is the direct successor to the Draft Programmatic Environmental Impact Statement for the Biological Defense Research Program (BDRP) promulgated by the Pentagon Neo-Cons during the Reagan administration that I had already analyzed, critiqued, and submitted to the Pentagon at the request of the Council for Responsible Genetics on 5 August 1988 (see Appendix I).[74] But this new 2004 FPEIS/CBDP admits that it is not a comprehensive, nationwide analysis of the Pentagon's complete CBDP. The 2004 FPEIS/CBDP admittedly excludes coverage of biowarfare work performed by the Pentagon's own Defense Advanced Research Projects Agency (DARPA). And of course the American people have little idea what the C.I.A. is really up to when it comes to biowarfare.

Even without taking into account the initiatives not made available for public knowledge and review, it is obvious from reading through the 2004 FPEIS/CBDP that the Pentagon is now gearing up to fight and "win" biological warfare pursuant to the September 2002 and December 2002 Bush Jr. national strategy directives mentioned above. Undoubtedly, the Central Intelligence Agency and DARPA are pursuing the same objectives. In particular FPEIS/CBDP paragraph 1.2.2.1 admits that in 2003 the mission of the CBDP was "expanded to cover military capability to operate in the face of threats in homeland security missions, *as well as warfighter missions*" (emphasis added):

> 1.2.2   Description of the Chemical and Biological Defense Program
> 1.2.2.1   Mission Objectives and Program Management
> Prior to 2003, the mission of the DoD CBDP was to provide world-class CB defense capabilities to allow U.S. military forces to survive and success-fully complete their operational missions in battlespace environments

> contaminated with CBW agents. In 2003, however, this mission expanded to cover military capability to operate in the face of threats in homeland security missions, *as well as warfighter missions.* . . . [Emphasis added.]

In 2003 the mission of the CBDP was revised in order to implement the above-mentioned September 2002 and December 2002 Bush Jr. first use national strategy directives. **The mission was revised in order to provide the Pentagon with the capability to launch *offensive* biological warfare and chemical warfare. Here it is: the proverbial smoking gun!** The offensive first use *policy* introduced by the Reagan/ Bush Jr. Neo-Conservatives in successive stages as outlined above is now coming to fruition in a new vastly expanded research and development *program* whose mission *has been altered* to permit development of *offensive capability in chemical and biological weapons*! Certainly that is the honest conclusion even a "friendly" foreign government will reach upon reading the FPEIS/CBDP without the need for adopting a "worst-case" analysis.

For further confirmation of this point, I contacted Ms. JoLane Souris, Environmental Coordinator, U.S. Army Medical Research and Material Command, at Fort Detrick, Maryland, whom Volume 68 of the Federal Register, No. 86, May 5, 2003, at page 23705 listed as the Pentagon's designated information contact person for the then Draft Programmatic Environmental Impact Statement for the CBDP. I asked her if the 2003 revision of the CBDP was a result of the Pentagon implementing the Bush Jr. September 2002 and December 2002 national strategy directives discussed above. She responded that this was "probably" the case. Reprinted below is a copy of this email correspondence:

From: Boyle, Francis [mailto:
FBOYLE@LAW.UIUC.EDU]
    Sent: Tuesday, May 03, 2005 4:23 PM
    TO: Boyle, Francis; Souris, JoLane D Ms
USAMRMC
    Subject: Question?
    Hi: I am going through the FPEIS for the
CBDP and have a question. paragraph 1.2.2.1
states that the mission of the CBDP was revised in
2003. I was wondering if that revision was the result
of the President's adoption of the new National
Security Directives of September 2002 and
December 2002?
    Thanks.
    fab.
    Francis A. Boyle
    Law Building
    504 E. Pennsylvania Ave.
    Champaign, IL 61820 USA
    217-333-7954 (voice)
    217-244-1478 (fax)
    fboyle@law.uiuc.edu
    (personal comments only)

    From: Souris, JoLane D Ms USAMRMC
[jolane.souris@us.army.mi]
    Sent: Wednesday, May 04, 2005 2:23 PM
    To: fboyle@law.uiuc.edu
    Subject: FW: Question?
    Follow Up Flag: Follow up
    Flag Status: Flagged
    Mr. Boyle,
    I did some research on this but have no
definitive answer. The CBDP Overview where this
came from merely stated the new mission
statement. I would think that the National Security
Directives probably did play in that change.
    ·JoLane

JoLane Souris, CHMM
USAMRMC Environmental Manager
MCMR-ZC-S
504 Scott Street
Fort Detrick, MD 21702-5012
301-619-2004
DSN 343-2004
Fax 301-619-6627

In follow-up email correspondence to me on 4 May 2005 at 2:48 p.m., Ms. Souris stated that this assessment was in part based upon "the information just told to us in interviews." I asked Ms. Souris to provide me with any documentation on this matter, which she kindly agreed to look into. On 12 May 2005, she informed me that she had no more information to report about my inquiry.

Even without this proverbial smoking gun, the Bush Jr. May 2004 FPEIS/CBDP looks strikingly similar to the snapshot picture of America's offensive biological warfare and chemical warfare programs taken by Seymour Hersh in his book *Chemical and Biological Warfare* (1968) when the United States had officially declared offensive biological warfare and chemical warfare programs. (Hersh published his seminal book just prior to President Nixon's 1969 Order against "bios.")

But the difference is this: the 1968 offensive component in itself was inadequate to give rise to the possibility of offensive use of biowarfare weapons, since the second primary component required to wage biowarfare—a program for defense of the civilian population, or more particularly, of its capacity to maintain the infrastructure needed for effective social order and functioning—was missing. Today, however, the Bush Jr. administration is concurrently developing a "civilian biodefense" industry that will provide the necessary concomitant for it to launch, wage, and "win" biological warfare. What was obviously near-suicidal and criminally irresponsible for President Nixon is now deemed to be eminently "doable" by President Bush Jr. and his Straussian Neo-Cons.[75]

But perhaps this is because public awareness that the preparation for offensive first use U.S. capability in biowarfare is now taking place appears to be minimal.

The Offensive Nature of "Civilian Defense"

As no state can embark upon a program of offensive use of biological weapons without taking steps to see that its civilian population is protected, the initiation of massive programs for civilian defense is necessarily a harbinger of an intent to deploy biowarfare.

That such programs differ from the normal and natural evolution of scientific development and public health protection is indicated by the difficulties besetting the U.S. effort to push them ahead. Despite the passage in 2004 of the $5.6 billion Project Bioshield bill designed to speed up drug companies' production of the specific drugs, diagnostic tools and vaccines called for by the Defense Science Board back in 2000, U.S. drug companies remained largely unresponsive: liability protection, guaranteed government purchases of bioterrorism drugs and greater government investment in research and development proved to be an insufficient incentive to spur new research and product development. Even with many of their financial and legal concerns addressed, the drug companies still failed to share the government's sense of overwhelming urgency. That skepticism was evident in a comment by Marie Vodicka, senior director for biologics and biotechnology of the Pharmaceutial Research and Manufacturers of America (PhRMA), that "Our companies are dedicated to meeting current health needs, and that has to be factored in when looking at the theoretical threats of the future."[76]

While such commitment to public health needs is surely admirable and deemed by PhRMA to be highly plausible as well, it hasn't followed the trend of Big Pharma elsewhere, particularly as it related to treatment of HIV/AIDS in Africa. More likely, it was simply indicative of the fact that at present there just is not enough profit to be made in such biowarfare work in order to seduce the drug companies.

But the government push is relentless. To bring the recalcitrant drug companies on board, new legislation has now been designed to sweeten the pot to intoxicating levels by, inter alia, extending existing patents on participating companies' most profitable unrelated products, leading to a windfall profit that could be worth billions.[77]

While U.S. military personnel have now been inoculated against anthrax and smallpox, and many U.S. health care workers against smallpox, the U.S. civilian population has refused to date to take the smallpox vaccines—decisions arrived at by thousands of people based on their own common sense assessment of the relative threat of terrorist attack compared to that of vaccination by a deleterious vaccine. After all, as the Centers for Disease Control reports on its website, smallpox was said to be "wiped out worldwide" in 1980, and "no cases of naturally occurring smallpox have happened since", with the virus kept in "two approved labs in the U.S. and Russia". This assessment of the current status of the disease is to be found on a CDC webpage titled "What You Should Know About a Smallpox Outbreak", which nonetheless seeks to provide counsel for public protection against the extinct disease, on the succinctly-worded and unsubstantiated grounds that "credible concern exists" that the virus might have been "made into a weapon by some countries and that terrorists may have obtained it."

For its part, the government is up to the minute on the pressing issue of protecting Americans against this disease under lock and key in American and Russian labs. On August 17th, the *Wall Street Journal* reported that the U.S. has "asked for bids for up to 80 million doses of a smallpox vaccine, with a potential value of more than $1.2 billion."[78] And just in case the public still doesn't understand the threat, it is currently preparing the legal architecture needed to force such dangerous vaccinations upon the American people when ordered on grounds of " public health " by manipulating public health laws.

The enormous amounts of money discussed above that the Bush Jr. administration is purportedly dedicating to "civilian defense" from a biowarfare attack, therefore, signal not only an effort to supposedly protect the civilian population from a threat whose foundation as yet remains unsubstantiated, but also betrays this administration's effort to be able to embark on offensive campaigns using biowarfare. Certainly the latter is the way foreign governments must and will analyze the burgeoning U.S. biowarfare "civilian defense" industry.

But it only makes perverse sense that the Bush Jr. administration is today preparing to defend America's civilian population from biowarfare retaliation by any adversary insofar as it has now officially announced America's new policy of adopting and implementing the aggressive first use of NBC/ WMD. It would be near-suicidal and certainly criminally irresponsible for the Bush Jr. administration to launch biowarfare as currently planned as of December 2002 without first having undertaken a massive program of biowarfare "civilian defense" for the American people, which is now dramatically and increasingly underway.

Of course, there has been no public discussion surrounding the possibility that the very programs which are ostensibly intended to safeguard against attacks can themselves serve as a vehicle to enable this rogue U.S. administration to unleash biowarfare attacks elsewhere in the world, with all the blowback that that portends. If the increasingly large public service sectors which were participating in the elaboration of civilian defense knew that they were in fact making preparations for the Bush Jr. administration to be able to deploy and use biological weapons on other peoples, and thereby *initiate or invite* a first-strike or retaliation, the sinister underpinnings of the program would arouse public revulsion, which might cripple further preparedness groundwork.

More Criminal Exposure for the CBDP

The totality of the Bush Jr. administration's pronounced policies and implementing programs on launching aggressive warfare by means of nuclear, biological and chemical weapons of mass destruction (NBC/WMD) places the United States government in breach of the Nuclear Non-Proliferation Treaty,

Biowarfare and Terrorism / Francis A. Boyle

the Biological Weapons Convention, and the Chemical Weapons Convention, as well as related U.S. domestic criminal legislation. The criminal nature of the Bush Jr.'s offensive strategies for the use of nuclear weapons has already been analyzed in my *The Criminality of Nuclear Deterrence* (2002) and *Destroying World Order* (2004), and so will not be repeated here. In a previous chapter, I have already discussed U.S. domestic criminal exposure for involvement in biowarfare activities under the BWC and the CRG's Biological Weapons Anti-Terrorism Act as currently amended. Here is the relevant U.S. law with respect to chemical weapons, found in Title 18 of the United States Code, Chapter 11B dealing with Chemical Weapons, Sections 229 and 229A, providing in relevant part as follows:

§ 229. Prohibited activities

(a) Unlawful conduct. –Except as provided in subsection (b), it shall be unlawful for any person knowingly—

(1) to develop, produce, otherwise acquire, transfer directly or indirectly, receive, stockpile, retain, own, possess, or use, or threaten to use, any chemical weapon; or

(2) to assist or induce, in any way, any person to violate paragraph (1), or to attempt to conspire to violate paragraph (1).

(b) Exempted agencies and persons. —

(1) In general. –Subsection (a) does not apply to the retention, ownership, possession, transfer, or receipt of a chemical weapon by a department, agency, or other entity of the United States, or by a person described in paragraph (2), pending destruction of the weapon.

. . . .

63

§ 229A. Penalties
(a) Criminal penalties. –
(1) In general. —Any person who violates section 229 of this title shall be fined under this title, or imprisoned for any term of years, or both.
(2) Death penalty. –Any person who violates section 229 of this title and by whose action the death of another person is the result shall be punished by death or imprisoned for life.

. . . .

When conjoined with the Chemical Weapons Convention, this U.S. domestic implementing legislation for that treaty creates—together with the BWC and its related CRG Act as revised—an extremely powerful package of combined international law and U.S. domestic criminal law that can be used to jam a second monkey-wrench into the Pentagon's CBDP.

Finally, United States Code Title 18, Chapter 113 B on Terrorism, Section 2332a is directly on point with respect to both chemical weapons and biological weapons, and thus provides lawyers, NGOs, and activists yet a third legal monkey-wrench to jam-up the works of the Pentagon's CBDP:

§ 2332a. Use of weapons of mass destruction
(a) Offense against a national of the United States or within the United States. –A person who, without lawful authority, uses, threatens, or attempts or conspires to use, a weapon of mass destruction—
(1) against a national of the United States while such national is outside of the United States;
(2) against any person or property within the United States, and
(A) the mail or any facility of interstate or foreign commerce

is used in furtherance of the offense;

(B) such property is used in interstate or foreign commerce or in an activity that affects interstate or foreign commerce;

(C) any perpetrator travels in or causes another to travel in interstate or foreign commerce in furtherance of the offense; or

(D) the offense, or the results of the offense, affect interstate or foreign commerce, or, in the case of a threat, attempt, or conspiracy, would have affected interstate or foreign commerce;

(3) against any property that is owned, leased or used by the United States or by any department or agency of the United States, whether the property is within or outside of the United States; or

(4) against any property within the United States that is owned, leased, or used by a foreign government, shall be imprisoned for any term of years or for life, and if death results, shall be punished by death or imprisoned for any term of years or for life.

(b) Offense by national of the United States outside of the United States. –Any national of the United States who, without lawful authority, uses, or threatens, attempts, or conspires to use, a weapon of mass destruction outside of the United States shall be imprisoned for any term of years or for life, and if death results, shall be punished by death, or by imprisonment for any term of years or for life.

(c) Definitions. –For purposes of this section—

. . . .

(2) the term "weapon of mass destruction" means—

(A) any destructive device as defined in section 921 of this title;

(B) any weapon that is designed or intended to cause death or serious bodily injury through the release, dissemination, or impact of toxic or poisonous chemicals, or their precursors;

(C) any weapon involving a biological agent, toxin, or vector (as those terms are defined in section 178 of this title); or

(D) any weapon that is designed to release radiation or radioactivity at a level dangerous to human life; and. . .

. . . .

Furthermore, Title 18 of the United States Code, Section 921(a)(4) defines a "destructive device" in relevant part as follows:

The term "destructive device" means—

(A) any explosive, incendiary, or poison gas—

(i) bomb.

(ii) grenade,

(iii) rocket having a propellant charge of more than four ounces,

(iv) missile having an explosive or incendiary charge of more than one-quarter ounce,

(v) mine, or

(vi) device similar to any of the devices described in the preceding clauses;

(B) any type of weapon. . . by whatever name known which will, or which may be readily converted to, expel a projectile by the action of an explosive or other propellant, and which has any barrel with a bore of more than one-half inch in diameter; and

(C) any combination of parts either designed or intended for use in converting any device into any destructive device described in subparagraph (A) or (B) and from which a destructive device may be readily assembled.

. . . .

Despite all of these stringent prohibitions set forth by both international treaties and United States domestic criminal law, in February of 2003 the United States government granted itself a patent on an illegal long-range biological weapons grenade that it has yet to relinquish despite a request by the NGO Sunshine Project to do so.[79]

Quite obviously, anyone currently involved in or contemplating getting involved with the Pentagon's CBDP has to ponder some heavy-duty legal exposure to severe criminal prosecution, up to and including the death penalty. Consequently, they had better seek non-governmental, independent, outside, and expert legal counsel from a qualified attorney at law immediately. The same conclusion applies to anyone engaged in or planning to get involved with biowarfare or chemical warfare work by the CIA and DAPRA, among other agencies of the U.S. government dealing directly with biological and chemical warfare.

67

Can World War III Be Far Behind?

By means of its twin national strategy directives of September 2002 and December 2002, the Bush Jr. administration made it crystal clear to the entire world that it will take forceful and aggressive military action by means of WMD against any state pursuing the exact same policies and practices with respect to nuclear, biological and chemical weapons of mass destruction that the Bush Jr. administration is currently implementing today. If this shoe were on the foot of some other state, the Bush Jr. administration would today be trumpeting around the world that effective action must be taken against the violator by the international community of states individually and collectively as well as by the United Nations Security Council and the U.N. General Assembly.

In actuality, that call of alarm is precisely what the Bush Jr. administration is most hypocritically and sanctimoniously undertaking today against Iran and North Korea under their respectively far less egregious circumstances. It was this very process that the Bush Jr. administration had most duplicitously perpetrated against Iraq starting in August of 2002—knowing full well that Iraq had no NBC/WMD to begin with. In fact, if a foreign adversary had indeed adopted the pronounced policies and implemented the programmatic capabilities that the Bush Jr. administration has already done with respect to NBC/WMD as articulated by the CBDP and otherwise, then pursuant to its national strategy directives of September 2002 and December 2002, the Bush Jr. administration would today be planning to launch an aggressive first strike against that target state by means of WMD. A fortiori Iran and North Korea.

Can World War III be far behind?

Bush Jr.'s Banana Republic

The Bush Jr. Neo-Cons swiftly manipulated these self-induced terrorist anthrax attacks upon the United States Congress to provide a public relations cover for launching a biowarfare arms race against the rest of the world in gross and material breach of the BWC—a campaign which they had originally intended to undertake two decades before, while working for the Reagan administration.[80] The Neo-Cons in the Bush Jr. administration have tried to sell this biowarfare arms race to the American people and the U.S. Congress as well as to the rest of the world by disingenuously claiming that it is all for the purpose of "defense," which, as previously explained, is not a permissible exception to the BWC in the first place.

Their specious argument deludes no one but the gullible, the frightened, the disinformed, the greedy, and the deliberately panicked. Certainly other major biotech states understand full well the military implications of this rapidly expanding U.S. biowarfare industry and will proceed to respond accordingly by deploying their own national biowarfare equivalents. The world will soon witness a de facto biological arms race among the major biotech states of the world under the guise of "defense", and despite the requirements of the BWC. The 1972 BWC itself will gradually fall into desuetude even if its skeleton is kept upon the law books—unlike its contemporaneous 1972 Anti-Ballistic Missile Systems (ABM) Treaty that the Bush Jr. Neo-Cons made a point of repudiating outright on 13 December 2001,[81] which they had also sought to accomplish going back to the Reagan administration,[82] but now using the 11 September 2001 terrorist attacks as a pretext for doing so.

It will then become only a matter of time before some state intelligence agency uses biological weapons again for domestic terrorist purposes or for foreign warfare; or else a catastrophic accident occurs at some biowarfare facility in the United States or abroad. In regard to this latter eventuality, the recent mass distribution—allegedly by mistake!—of a virulent 1957 pandemic flu virus strain which killed between 1 million and 4 million people to 4,614 laboratories primarily in the United States and also to seventeen foreign countries is a harbinger of things to come.[83]

The massive proliferation of biowarfare technology, facilities, as well as trained scientists and technicians all over the United States courtesy of the Neo-Con Bush Jr. administration will render a catastrophic biowarfare or bioterrorist incident or accident a statistical certainty. If such a catastrophic event should occur, it would mark the final end to democracy, human rights, the rule of law, and the Constitution in the United States of America even as we know and experience it today, as materially diminished under the burgeoning Bush Jr. Neo-Con police state.

Indicative of its awareness of just such a possibility, the Bush administration admitted in 2002 that plans for a shadow government had been drawn up, to be activated in the event of such a catastrophe; its level of commitment to future democracy was clearly indicated by the fact that then Senate Majority leader, Tom Daschle (Democrat) had not even been informed of such a plan. As far as the perpetrators of such a catastrophe event are concerned, at such a point, it would hardly matter—if it were ever to be found out—whether they were foreigners or Americans. But no matter: as President Bush Jr. ominously stated shortly before the terrorist attacks of 11 September 2001: "A dictatorship would be a heck of a lot easier, there's no question about it."[84]

We still have time to head off Constitutional extinction and biological Armageddon:

. . . .
O say, does that star-spangled banner yet wave
O'er the land of the free and the home of the
brave?

. . . .

The answer to that question is in the hands of the American people.[85]

CHAPTER EIGHT

REINING IN BIOWARFARE RESEARCH:

HOW IT CAN BE DONE / WHY WE MUST DO IT

No Escape for U.S. in Misinterpreting BWC Obligations

Article 31, paragraph 1 of the seminal 1969 Vienna Convention of the Law of Treaties sets forth the general rule of customary international law for the interpretation of a treaty such as the Biological Weapons Convention in the following language:

> A treaty shall be interpreted in good faith in accordance with the ordinary meaning to be given to the terms of the treaty in their context and in the light of its object and purpose.

Quite obviously, the United States government is deliberately interpreting and applying the BWC:

(1) In bad faith;

71

(2) In accordance with a tortured and tortuous meaning of the BWC's prima facie "terms";

(3) In violation of its own domestic implementing legislation for the BWC, which provides an authoritative interpretation of the requirements of the BWC as far as the United States of America is concerned, both under public international law as well as under U.S. domestic constitutional law and criminal law; and

(4) The United States government is implementing this perverse interpretation of the BWC in order to defeat both the "object" and the "purpose" of the BWC.

In part, the "object and purpose" of the BWC can be located within its preambular paragraphs. In particular, I want to draw special attention to the following language taken from the Preamble to the BWC:

The States Parties to this Convention,

Determined to act with a view to achieving effective progress towards general and complete disarmament, including the prohibition and elimination of all types of weapons of mass destruction, and convinced that the prohibition of the development, production and stockpiling of chemical and bacteriological (biological) weapons and their elimination, through effective measures, will facilitate the achievement of general and complete disarmament under strict and effective international control,

. . . .

Convinced of the importance and urgency of eliminating from the arsenals of

States, through effective measures, such dangerous weapons of mass destruction as those using chemical or bacteriological (biological) agents,

. . . .

Determined, for the sake of all mankind, to exclude completely the possibility of bacteriological (biological) agents and toxins being used as weapons,

Convinced that such use would be repugnant to the conscience of mankind and that no effort should be spared to minimize this risk,

Have agreed as follows:

. . . .

Notice that in accordance with the BWC and the rule of customary international law set forth in Article 31(1) of the Vienna Convention on the Law of Treaties, one general test for whether any particular component of the massive U.S. biowarfare program instituted by the Bush Jr. administration after 9/11 is lawful and thus not criminal is whether that component will "exclude completely the possibility of bacteriological (biological) agents and toxins being used as weapons." The second general test is whether any such component will "minimize this risk" of biological agents and toxins "being used as weapons."

However, for numerous components of the current U.S. biowarfare program, the contrary is true on either one or both grounds. In fact, the Bush Jr. administration has set out to violate and defeat both the "object" and the "purpose" of the BWC itself. The Bush Jr. administration's biowarfare policies, practices, and programs will turn the BWC into a legal nullity.

It is clear that today the United States government stands in "material breach" of the BWC as determined by and subject to the rules of customary international law set forth in Article 60 of the Vienna Convention on the Law of Treaties:

. . . .

2.   A material breach of a multilateral treaty by one of the parties entitles:

(a) The other parties by unanimous agreement to suspend the operation of the treaty in whole or in part or terminate it either:

(i) In the relations between themselves and the defaulting State, or

(ii) As between all the parties;

(b) A party specially affected by the breach to invoke it as a ground for suspending the operation of the treaty in whole or in part in the relations between itself and the defaulting State;

(c) Any party other than the defaulting State to invoke the breach as a ground for suspending the operation of the treaty in whole or in part with respect to itself if the treaty is of such a character that a material breach of its provisions by one party radically changes the position of every party with respect to the further performance of its obligations under the treaty.

3. A material breach of a treaty, for the purposes of this article, consists in:

(a)   A repudiation of the treaty not sanctioned by the present Convention; or

(b)   The violation of a provision essential to the accomplishment of the object or purpose of the treaty.

4. The foregoing paragraphs are without prejudice to any provision in the treaty applicable in the event of a breach.

. . . .

Activating the Biological Weapons Convention's Complaint Procedure

International treaties sometimes include provisions for recourse, should a state party violate the treaty. Further to the above-quoted Article 60(4) of the Vienna Convention on the Law of Treaties, BWC Article VI provides:

> (1) Any State Party to this Convention which finds that any other State Party is acting in breach of obligations deriving from the provisions of the Convention may lodge a complaint with the Security Council of the United Nations. Such a complaint should include all possible evidence confirming its validity, as well as a request for its consideration by the Security Council.
>
> (2) Each State Party to this Convention undertakes to cooperate in carrying out any investigation which the Security Council may initiate, in accordance with the provisions of the Charter of the United Nations, on the basis of the complaint received by the Council. The Security Council shall inform the States Parties to the Convention of the results of the investigation.

In recognition of the dire hazard that biowarfare research, development and deployment poses to the future of humanity, and in the face of the potential exacerbation of an international arms race for bioweapons development flowing from U.S. actions, it is incumbent upon states parties to the BWC to "lodge a complaint with the Security Council" against the United States and demand an "investigation" under BWC Article VI.

The Security Council is furthermore authorized to undertake such an "investigation" in accordance with its powers under Chapter VI of the U.N. Charter dealing with the Pacific Settlement of Disputes. In particular, U.N. Charter Article 34 provides:

> The Security Council may investigate any dispute, or any situation which might lead to international friction or give rise to a dispute, in order to determine whether the continuance of the dispute or situation is likely to endanger the maintenance of international peace and security.

According to U.N. Charter Article 27(3), it would require nine affirmative votes on the fifteen-member Security Council to initiate such a BWC Article VI investigation against the United States, which would be obligated to abstain from the voting because it would be a party to the dispute:

> Decisions of the Security Council on all other matters [i.e., non-procedural] shall be made by an affirmative vote of nine members including the concurring votes of the permanent members; provided that, in decisions under Chapter VI . . . a party to a dispute shall abstain from voting.

In the event the United States government tried to prevent the initiation of such a BWC Article VI investigation by the Security Council, then this bad faith conduct would directly open up the Withdrawal Clause of BWC Article XIII (2) for exercise by any and every state party to the BWC:

> Each State Party to this Convention shall in exercising its national sovereignty have the right to withdraw from the Convention if it decides that extraordinary events, related to the subject matter of the Convention, have jeopardized the supreme interests of its country. It shall give notice of such withdrawal to all other States Parties to the Convention and to the United Nations Security Council three months in advance. Such notice shall include a statement

of the extraordinary events it regards as having
jeopardized its supreme interests.

In this case the "extraordinary events" that "jeopardized"
the "supreme interests" of the BWC states parties would be
the Bush Jr. biowarfare programs coupled with and compounded
by its stonewalling of a Security Council investigation pursuant
to a valid "complaint" filed by a BWC state party under BWC
Article VI as well as under U.N. Charter Article 35(1): "Any
Member of the United Nations may bring any dispute, or any
situation of the nature referred to in Article 34, to the attention
of the Security Council or the General Assembly."

Filing a BWC Complaint for Investigation
by the U.N. Secretary-General

Furthermore, states parties to the BWC should also file
a formal complaint against the United States with the U.N.
Secretary-General under the authority of U.N. Security Council
Resolution 620(26 Aug. 1988), which:

> . . . .
> 2. Encourages the Secretary-General to carry
> out promptly investigations in response to
> allegations brought to his attention by any
> Member State concerning the possible use
> of chemical and bacteriological (biological)
> or toxic weapons that may constitute a
> violation of the 1925 Geneva Protocol or other
> relevant rules of customary international law,
> in order to ascertain the facts of the matter,
> and to report the results;
>
> . . . .

The U.N. Secretary-General is obliged to conduct a formal
investigation of such a complaint pursuant to the procedures
set forth in U.N. Doc. A/44/561 (4 Oct. 1989) as called for by
U.N. General Assembly Resolution 42/37C (30 Nov. 1987).

In Working Paper BWC/CONF.V/COW/WP.17 submitted by the United States to the Fifth Review Conference of the BWC states parties for their formal adoption, which was dated 26 November 2001—that is, right after the terrorist anthrax attacks on the U.S. Congress—the Bush Jr. administration officially took the position that these aforementioned complaint and investigation procedures applied to allegations concerning both the use and the threat of use of biological or toxin weapons, stating:

> The States Parties reaffirm their agreement to consult, at the request of any State Party, regarding allegations of use or threat of use of bacteriological (biological) or toxin weapons and to cooperate fully with the United Nations Secretary-General in carrying out such investigations.

The Bush Jr. National Strategy Directives of September 2002 and December 2002 conjoined with the Pentagon's FPEIS/CBDP of May 2004 brazenly threaten every state in the world community with the criminal first use of biological weapons. The Bush Jr. administration stands in anticipatory breach of the 1925 Geneva Protocol as well as of the BWC.

Hoisting the Bush Jr. Administration With Its Own Petard

In regard to filing these BWC complaints against the United States with the U.N. Security Council and with the U.N. Secretary-General, the BWC complaining states parties should invoke and use the U.S. government's own official interpretation of these BWC complaint procedures and requirements as set forth in that aforementioned Working Paper that the Bush Jr. administration submitted to the Fifth Review Conference of the BWC states parties on 26 November 2001 for their formal adoption:

Proposals
Working paper by the United States of America

. . . .

ARTICLE VI

1. The conference notes that the provisions of this Article have not been invoked.

2. The Conference reaffirms the importance of Article VI, which, in addition to the procedures contained in Article V, provides that any State Party which finds that any other State Party is acting in breach of its obligations under the Convention may lodge a complaint with the United Nations Security Council. The Conference emphasizes the provision of Article VI that such a complaint should include all possible evidence confirming its validity. It stresses that, as in the case of the implementation of all the provisions and procedures set forth in the Convention, the procedures foreseen in Article VI should be implemented in good faith within the scope of the Convention.

3. The Conference invites the Security Council to consider immediately any complaint lodged under Article VI and to initiate any measures it considers necessary for the investigation of the complaint in accordance with the Charter. The Conference reaffirms the undertaking of each State Party to cooperate in carrying out any investigations which the Security Council may initiate.

4. The Conference recalls, in this context, United Nations Security Council resolution 620 (1988), which at the time encouraged the United Nations Secretary-General to carry out prompt investigations, in response to allegations brought to its attention by any Member State concerning the possible use

of chemical and bacteriological (biological) or toxin weapons that could entail a violation of the 1925 Geneva Protocol or of any other applicable rule of international treaty or customary law. The Conference also recalls the technical guidelines and procedures contained in Annex I of United Nations document A/44/561 to guide the United Nations Secretary-General on the timely and efficient investigation of reports of the possible use of such weapons. The States Parties reaffirm their agreement to consult, at the request of any State Party, regarding allegations of use or threat of use of bacteriological (biological) or toxin weapons and to cooperate fully with the United Nations Secretary-General in carrying out such investigations. The Conference stresses that in the case of alleged use the United Nations is called upon to take appropriate measures expeditiously, which could include a request to the Security Council to consider action in accordance with the Charter.

5. The Conference invites the Security Council to inform each State Party of the results of any investigation initiated under Article VI and to consider promptly any appropriate further action which may be necessary.

6. The Conference notes that the procedure outlined in this Article is without prejudice to the prerogative of the States Parties to the Convention to consider jointly the cases of alleged non-compliance with the provisions of the Convention and to make appropriate decisions in accordance with the Charter of the United Nations and applicable rules of international law.

The BWC states parties should use the United States' own official interpretation of the legal obligations under BWC article VI to support their BWC complaints against the United States before the U.N. Security Council and with the U.N. Secretary-General, throughout the entirety of the United Nations Organization, and around the world at large.

In order to trigger and expedite these U.N. complaint procedures, BWC states parties can simply transmit this book to both the U.N. Security Council and to the U.N. Secretary-General with letters of transmittal demanding investigations on the basis of the evidence set forth herein and as required by the international and U.S. domestic legal authorities specified above. The author is prepared to assist any BWC state party in drafting those complaints/letters of transmittal to the U.N. Security Council and to the U.N. Secretary-General pro bono publico. This book has been written in order to state the legal case against the Bush Jr. administration's biowarfare policies, programs, and practices under both international law and U.S. domestic law. NGOs and activists in all BWC states parties can use this book to pressure their respective governments into filing those complaints with the U.N. Security Council and the U.N. Secretary-General.

Further Recourse Through the U.N. General Assembly

If the United States government successfully sabotages or stonewalls BWC investigations by the U.N. Security Council or by the U.N. Secretary-General, then the complaining BWC state party can bring its Article VI complaint against the United States to the U.N. General Assembly for action under U.N. Charter Article 35(1), quoted above. Depending upon the precise details of the procedural posture of this BWC complaint to the General Assembly, it might be possible for the U.N. General Assembly to sanction the United States pursuant to the terms of its pathbreaking Uniting for Peace Resolution 377(A)(V) of 3 November 1950.

It is high time for the world community of states and especially the BWC contracting states parties to formally confront the United States of America on the Bush Jr. biowarfare programs in order to prevent the gradual disintegration of the Biological Weapons Convention as other states scramble to launch their own countermeasures designed to counteract this wholesale pattern of BWC violations by the Bush Jr. administration. Time is of the essence. Humanity is at risk.

A Warning to Scientists

Toward that end, in the summer of 1990, I drafted, published and widely circulated a "Warning" to scientists about getting involved in biological warfare research. [86] That warning bears repetition today. As indicated therein, American scientists whose "research" projects violate the terms of the BWC and its domestic implementing legislation, the Biological Weapons Anti-Terrorism Act, can be held legally accountable for their actions. This was and is intended not merely to warn scientists of the threat of legal action—an undertaking much more plausibly to be undertaken by American citizens due to the domestic legal recourse afforded by the 1989 domestic implementing legislation for the BWC as currently amended— but also to put this option forward for possible pursuit by concerned members of the public, who may wish to call for legal action in relation to particular violations which have come to their attention:

A WARNING TO SCIENTISTS

This is to inform all life science researchers that on May 22, 1990, President George Bush signed into law the Biological Weapons Anti-terrorism Act of 1989, Public Law Number 101-298, which implements the terms of the Biological Weapons Convention of 1972. Generally put, this Act provides that anyone subject to the jurisdiction of the United States who "knowingly develops, produces,

---

> stockpiles, transfers, acquires, retains, or possesses any biological agent, toxin, or delivery system for use as a weapon, or knowingly assists a foreign state or any organization to do so, shall be fined under this title *or imprisoned for life* or any term of years, or both." In my professional opinion, many research projects that have already been funded by the Department of Defense's so-called Biological Defense Research Program (BDRP) raise serious compliance problems with the Biological Weapons Convention and thus with this Act. Therefore, if you are currently receiving, or contemplating applying for, BDRP research funds, you should obtain legal advice and counsel from a competent attorney as to whether or not you should proceed with your research or grant application. Remember that a violation of this Act could subject you to life imprisonment! Hence, I recommend that you proceed with extreme caution when dealing with the Department of Defense, and especially with its BDRP.

It would be my advice that concerned citizens, activists, and NGOs circulate this "Warning" far and wide throughout the United States and especially to America's entire life-science community, relevant journals, and local newspapers.

Campaign for the Peaceful Development of the Biological Sciences

In June of 2004 the Council for Responsible Genetics launched a Campaign for the Peaceful Development of the Biological Sciences set forth below. Their Statement not only indicates the potential hazards that lie ahead if action is not taken, but also enumerates a series of actions to be taken. Signatories to date, a means to sign the petition, and other relevant information can presently be found on the CRG website at <http://www.gene-watch.org>. You can get personally involved in this monumental struggle against the Bush Jr. biowarfare programs there.

Campaign for the Peaceful Development of the Biological Sciences

By the Council for Responsible Genetics (CRG)

30 June 2004

We, the undersigned are deeply concerned by the current expansion of United States research on biological weapons agents. With the stated aim of developing vaccines, therapeutics, and diagnostic tools to defend civilian populations against bioterrorism, the United States has entered uncharted territory. We believe that the current biodefense expansion has the potential to seriously threaten public safety, international security, and the vitality of open biomedical research, and to drain scarce resources from key public health programs.

The purpose of the 1972 Biological Weapons Convention (BWC) is to "exclude completely the possibility of bacteriological (biological) agents and toxins being used as weapons" by prohibiting the development, production, stockpiling, acquisition, and retention of such weapons. However, a substantial area of "defensive" research involves activities that are indistinguishable

---

from those conducted for offensive purposes. For example, efforts to diagnose and treat exposure to biological weapons necessarily involve their production and dispersal. Therefore, states must provide concrete transparency measures to verify their defensive intent. The United States has undermined such efforts, by rejecting an inspection and verification protocol to the BWC, and has since embarked on a sweeping expansion in its biological defense research. This research includes efforts to explore the properties of novel biological agents with enhanced offensive characteristics in the name of "threat assessment." We believe that the present construction of over a dozen new high-containment laboratories across the country that will handle potential biological warfare agents will further undermine the United States' commitment to biological disarmament.

The proliferation of these laboratories greatly increases the likelihood of accidental and intentional releases that could threaten public safety and security. Technological improvements in the design of these facilities may reduce, but cannot hope to eliminate, the consequences of human error and wrongdoing. Bhopal and Three Mile Island are only a few of the many disastrous incidents that experts never anticipated. The knowledge and access to resources these facilities create can also be dangerously misused. As the 2001 anthrax mailings showed, biodefense laboratories have become a source of home grown terrorism.

Infectious diseases such as influenza, tuberculosis, hepatitis, malaria,

SARS, and HIV/AIDS represent a global public health crisis of the highest order, to which the United States must urgently respond. In such a climate, the growing diversion of needed public health resources toward speculative threats should be approached with the greatest skepticism. We believe that inflated and poorly substantiated claims of catastrophic bioterrorism have been marshaled to justify this diversion.

At the same time, we are deeply troubled by the specter of secrecy and security restrictions in biomedical research. Open disclosure is critical to maintaining public confidence in the integrity of scientific work. Censorship and classification of research, not seen at this scale since the Cold War era in physics, strike at the core of fundamental values and at academic freedom, the advancement of knowledge, and the use of public funds for public benefits. These new policies have not been backed by clear and specific threats associated with the dissemination of scientific findings.

We therefore call for the following:

1. A moratorium on the current proliferation of new biological defense laboratories, whose missions do not serve a compelling public health purpose;

2. A rejection of the proposed multi-billion dollar biodefense spending initiative for the development of drugs and vaccines to defend against potential biological weapons, and a redirection of such spending toward pressing public health needs;

3. A prohibition against the development of novel biological and toxic agents, or the modification of biological agents, to enhance virulence, pathogenicity, or transmission characteristics, for any purposes, including biological defense;

4. A reversal of efforts to classify basic research in biology, whether that research is conducted by government, university, or private actors;

5. The creation of mandatory public reporting requirements for all accidents, including laboratory infections, environmental releases and breaches of security, at Biosafety Level 2, 3 and 4 facilities across the country;

6. The full disclosure of minutes from all institutional biosafety committees in universities and other institutions involved in biological defense research.

7. A reaffirmation of commitment to the Biological Weapons Convention and to the Nuremberg Principles, according to which acting under the direction of a government does not relieve people of their responsibilities under international law.

A LETTER OF DEMAND TO THE DEPARTMENT OF DEFENSE ON THE CBDP FINAL PROGRAMMATIC ENVIRONMENTAL IMPACT STATEMENT

Introduction

One of the nice things about being a law professor is that if you really do not like something that is going on in the world you can always file a lawsuit in order to do something about it. Toward that end, after I had reviewed the Final Programmatic Environmental Impact Statement (FPEIS) for the

Pentagon's Chemical and Biological Defense Program (CBDP) of May 2004, I contacted my colleague and friend, Mr. Terry Lodge, Esq. of Toledo, Ohio, who is an expert on environmental law. After Mr. Lodge read my analysis of the Pentagon's FPEIS/CBDP, he recommended that we start the process by filing a formal complaint with the Pentagon to the effect that its FPEIS/CBDP has not complied with the reporting requirements of the National Environmental Policy Act (NEPA). Set forth below is the text of our joint Complaint that we filed with the Pentagon on 25 August 2005.

We have not yet heard back from the Pentagon. On the other hand, so far the Pentagon has not yet signed off on and approved the FPEIS/CBDP. The proverbial "ball" is now in the Pentagon's "court." Mr. Lodge and I will continue to ride herd on the situation and will take further appropriate legal action as indicated by the developing circumstances. In the meantime, readers are urged to organize grassroots movements in your local communities in order to prevent or at least to stop any type of CBDP programs that are proposed or are already ongoing by using this Complaint and these objections that have already been filed by Mr. Lodge and me with the Pentagon.

✻

Law Offices Of
Terry Jonathan Lodge
316 N. Michigan St., Ste. 520
Toledo, Ohio 43624-1627
(419) 255-7552
Fax (419) 255-8582

August 25, 2005

Claude M. Bolton, Jr.
Office of the Assistant Secretary of the Army
Acquisition, Logistics and Technology Affairs
103 Army Pentagon
Washington, D.C. 20310-0103

Via fax to 703-614-7372 (or to alternate fax 703-614-7372) and overnight mail

Re: Final Programmatic Environmental Impact Statement on the Department of Defense Chemical and Biological Defense Program (May 2004)

Dear Assistant Secretary Bolton:

We are Francis A. Boyle, a Professor of International Law at the University of Illinois in Champaign, and Terry J. Lodge, longtime environmental attorney.

Professor Boyle drafted the U.S. domestic implementing legislation for the 1972 Convention on the Prohibition of the Development, Production and Stockpiling of Bacteriological (Biological) and Toxin Weapons and on Their Destruction, that is commonly known as the Biological Weapons Anti-Terrorism Act of 1989, Public Law No. 101-298 (1990), that was passed unanimously by both Houses of the U.S. Congress and signed into law by President George H. W. Bush and is currently codified at 18 United States Code §§ 175-78.

We offer the following comments on the Department of Defense's May 2004 draft "Final Programmatic Environmental Impact Statement (hereinafter FPEIS}" for the "Chemical and Biological Defense Program (CBDP)". We understand that it is your responsibility to execute the Record of Decision on the FPEIS. While we are submitting our comments beyond the deadline for such to have been made according to the DoD's circular announcing the Draft PEIS/CBDP, we are taking advantage of the DoD's having not finalized the FPEIS to ask that you reconsider many serious flaws with the FPEIS that demonstrate lack of compliance with the letter and spirit of the National Environmental Policy Act of 1970. We ask specifically that in light of the new information we have conveyed in this letter that signing of the ROD be indefinitely shelved and a Supplemental Environmental Impact Statement be compiled.

As a general observation, the FPEIS masks or obscures certain putatively illegal biowarfare components of the CBDP that violate both international and domestic law, including but not limited to the Biological Weapons Convention and the Biological Weapons Anti-Terrorism Act of 1989 as currently amended, and further that the FPEIS gives cover to possible deleterious and detrimental environmental consequences of implementation of the CBDP. It appears that pursuant to the redirection of military policies and plans by the Bush Administration that the DoD is focused on developing chemical and biological weapons as a "deterrent" to CBW threats from elsewhere, *i.e.,* that the purpose is to maintain and expand an offensive-use program. A reasonable reading of the draft and final FPEIS documents certainly supports the conclusion that the Department of Defense is moving toward the development of CBW "deterrents," which would be illegal under the terms of the BWC.

We itemize as follows:

1) According to paragraph 1.2.2.1 in 2003 the mission of the DoD CBDP was "expanded to cover military capabilities to operate in the face of threats in homeland security missions, as well as to warfighter missions."[1] It appears that the mission has probably been expanded to take into account the new White House national strategy documents on preventive warfare, even by means of weapons of mass destruction, including biological weapons. Please clarify and explain.

2) In paragraph 1.3.2, DoD admits that it is engaged in outdoor aerosol testing with simulants of genetically-engineered microorganisms that have been intentionally modified by alteration of genetic information. This appears to describe testing of the dispersal of GEM bioweapons. Please clarify and explain.

3) In paragraph 1.3.3 DoD states that it did not examine all CBDP activities at all sites in detail for preparation of the FPEIS. This suggests that the FPEIS is incomplete. Moreover, paragraph 2.1 indicates that the last comprehensive review was the BDRP final programmatic environmental impact statement of April 1989, so some of the information being

relied upon in 2004-2005 is quite dated, if not wholly out of date. Please clarify and explain.

4) In paragraph 2.2.1.1 is the statement that "medical systems prototypes such as vaccines are tested using human volunteers." This tends to evidence active preparation for use in hostilities. Please clarify and explain.

5) According to paragraph 2.3.4.3, under the Federal Clean Water Act it is unlawful to discharge any radiological, chemical, or biological warfare agent, any high level radioactive waste or any medical waste into navigable waters. But this prohibition does not apply to non-navigable waters. The FPEIS does not address the question whether such waste is being discharged into non-navigable waters. Please clarify and explain.

6) According to paragraph 2.3.5.1, safety practices and procedures for laboratory work with genetically engineered microorganisms are detailed within the guidelines for research involving recombinant DNA molecules, NIH 2002.

However, the army established regulations involving the use of etiologic agents in research activities by DA and its contractors mandating adherence to the CDC/NIH guidelines and providing further safety requirements, including AR385-69, Biological Defense Safety Program, December 1993. Thus before work involving etiologic agents by DA activities and army contractors can commence, a hazard analysis and job safety evaluation are required by AR385-69. Has this been done?

7) At the Edgewood Chemical Biological Center (ECBC, mentioned in paragraph 2.4.1), the MacNamara Life Sciences Building (*see* paragraph 2.4.1.1.b) has inhalation suites. Edgewood does have a BSL-3 laboratory. It also has aerosol testing using indoor laboratory facilities. Pigs are used in testing there, and pigs have a circulatory and respiratory system akin to that of human beings.

The FPEIS contains an admission that they have worked with genetically engineered microorganisms at Edgewood, but not as part of the CBDP. Then at whose behest were they doing this work? The Defense Advanced Research Projects Agency (DARPA)? The Central Intelligence Agency?

The etiologic agents studied at ECBC within the CBDP comprise a variety of toxins and organisms of military interest, including bacteria, viruses and rickettsia. Live BSL-3 agents were not used in CBDP-related activities at ECBC in 2000 and 2001. But what about 2002, 2003, and 2004? And what about non-CBDP related activities with distinct bioweapons implications undertaken by "other" agencies? Do such references mean the CIA? Such facts must be disclosed if there is to be a meaningful opportunity for public comment and participation under NEPA.

8) At paragraph 2.4.2, U.S. Army Medical Research Institute of Chemical Defense (paragraph 2.4.2.1.f) says that GEMs are not used during CBDP related activities at USAMRICD. But what about non-CBDP related activities? And what about non-CBDP activities involving the use of human subjects? No express statement appears here, only one that is highly conditioned. It is imperative to disclose the extent and nature of "other-agency", possibly DARPA or CIA, activities.

9) At page 2-46 is a statement that the principal investigator must prepare and submit protocols involving DNA research to the USAMRICD institutional biosafety committee for review, evaluation, and approval (page 2-49). This constitutes an admission that staff at the facility are working with cultures and toxins associated with botulism. For what purpose?

10) There is an indication (paragraph 2.4.3) that non-CBDP activities are also being conducted at the Naval Surface Warfare Center Dahlgren Laboratory (page 2-53). Does this reference, too, refer to DARPA or the CIA, or both? The agents being used in the BSL-3 lab include ricin, botulinum toxin, yersinia pestis and anthrax (page 2-54). It says that GEMS are not used in CBDP activities at NSWCDL, but there is no explanation of the nature of non-CBDP activities. Please clarify and explain.

11) With reference to paragraph 2.4.4, which mentions the U.S. Army Medical Research Institute of Infectious Diseases located at Fort Detrick, Maryland, at page 2-61 there is an indication that the U.S. Department of Agriculture also has facilities at Fort Detrick. For what purpose?

According to subparagraph 2.4.4.l.e, vaccine development relies heavily on RDNA work.

At page 2-74 it states that a worker who cannot be immunized for medical reasons when a vaccine is available for an etiologic agent is not permitted to work with that agent and is not allowed in any laboratory where work with that agent is being conducted. This apparently means that vaccines are essentially mandatory, which raises the question of how voluntary any of these vaccines really are. Do these vaccines violate the Nuremberg Code on Medical Experimentation, which has been incorporated into DOD Regulations? Please clarify and explain.

12) FPEIS paragraph 2.4.5, referencing Dugway Proving Ground, indicates that DPG's primary mission is to plan, conduct, analyze the results of exploratory, developmental and production tests of CB defense systems, smoke and obscure illumination material, and delivery systems. However, delivery systems are clearly illegal under federal law and treaty. Yet the description in this section is of the development and production of CB systems as well as delivery systems. Please clarify and explain.

13) The mention of "pads" at pages 2-78 and 2-79 is suspect. These pads are used to study how a chemical agent is transferred onto an object; hence there apparently is ongoing study of how to optimize offensive chemical weapons use.

14) At FPEIS page 2-80 is a statement that GEMS are not used in CBDP activities at Dugway, but what about DARPA or the CIA? There is no disclosure of the identity of GEMS users there.

15) At page 2-82 there is a description of discharge of toxic fluids into groundwater. Effluent from a lagoon at Dugway is conveyed into an open ditch, which out-falls into a pond and run-off area west of the lagoon. The other three waste water lagoons are considered permitted by rule, which exempts them from UDWQ's requirement of a groundwater discharge permit. The obvious conclusion is that they just discharge their waste water into groundwater. Please justify.

16) At page 2-83 is found reference to release of biological or chemical agents into the open air. This is strictly prohibited by federal law, *see* 50 U.S.C. § 1512.[2]

17) At FPEIS page 2-84 it states that organisms that are BLS-3 or lower and that have been improved through the environmental and test review process can be used for BD testing at Dugway. The LSTF is the only DPG facility where biological agents can be used for testing purposes.

18) At page 2-88 it states that some chemical agents are sent directly to DPG by the test customer. Who are all test customers? The failure to provide this information deprives the public of the opportunity for meaningful comment.

19) At page 2-101 is an indication that the BSL-3 laboratories of Battelle Memorial Institute, located at West Jefferson, Ohio provide floor space for work with anthrax, botulinum toxin, plague and tularemia. Vaccine testing using the actual pathogens or toxins is limited to those agents. The dedicated floor space indicates that these agents might be subjected to dual-use offensive/defensive purposes, which is clearly prohibited by law. Please clarify and explain.

20) Under Section 5, "Analysis of Environmental and Health Consequences of Chemical and Biological Defense Program Activities and Mitigation Measures," at page 5-28 is the explanation that the FPEIS will provide a basis for tiering of future environmental analyses under the CBDP which will

facilitate future government decision-making as the program grows to meet "evolving threats". Thus there is a bald admission that the CBDP is going to expand and that, indeed, there are already firm plans for it. There is no definition nor delineation of the "evolving threats", nor any explanation which would justify the expansion of the CBDP. This deprives the public of vital information for meaningful comment.

21) In Attachment A 3 dated November 2000 at (D) is an indication that on June 13, 2000 the BDRP process was expanded "into an environmental impact statement of the chemical as well as biological defense programs." Is that true of the 2003 Revision? Please clarify and explain.

22) In Appendix B, page B7 in correspondence from the U.S. Department of the Interior to the Pentagon dated June 16, 2003 it says: "Numerous contaminants from test pathogens, pharmaceuticals and hormones used in both research and in the care of animals are found in the waste products" at Fort Detrick. Please clarify and explain.

23) At Appendix C, entitled "Hazard Analyses" at page C-1 is a description of the generation, release and downwind transport of potentially hazardous biological or chemical material as major aspects of the testing program. The aerosol and vapor forms are the physical states most apt for a biological or chemical agent to escape. There is no explanation of how this potentially lethal activity would be controlled or mitigated. Please clarify and explain.

24) At page C-2 is a description of a computer program developed to model NBC and radiological and high explosive collateral effects resulting from conventional weapons strikes against potential target facilities. It states that the purpose of this program is to anticipate enemy weapons of mass destruction, but this computer program is "dual use" in that it could also be used by the U.S. for offensive purposes. Please clarify and explain. The program is based upon a maximum credible event (MCE), but appears not to have considered

someone flying a jumbo jet into Fort Detrick, or analysis of the anthrax outbreak at Sverdlovsk, or even the anthrax attacks on the U.S. Congress, which used Fort Detrick anthrax. Please clarify and explain.

25) At page C-6 is a statement that private couriers are used for transport of etiologic agents used in the CBDP, rather than the U.S. Postal Service—in other words, Federal Express and UPS. This affords considerable opportunity for such agents to be lost—witness the influenza test dissemination earlier in 2005. Please clarify and explain.

26) The mention at page C-7 that the CBDP has a special tick laboratory means that the DoD is experimenting with how to use ticks for biological warfare purposes. Please clarify and explain.

27) At page C-9 is mention of terrorist attacks including airplane crashes, but there appears to be no MCE analysis of it; hence there is no analysis of a 9/11-style attack on Fort Detrick, nor of anthrax attacks on Congress with Fort Detrick anthrax. There is mention of the use of anthrax-contaminated letters, which by the time this report was released in May of 2004 had been identified as coming from Fort Detrick. Yet even this MCE was not analyzed, either. Please clarify and explain.

28) At page C-10 is narrative recognizing the various methods of dissemination of simulants in outdoor tests, including aerial spray from aircraft or tethered balloons, spray from ground vehicles, explosives dissemination, air cannon and various atomization devices. Thus it may be reasonably concluded that the CBDP has been engaging in research, development, testing, and evaluation of all of these types of delivery systems and dispersal mechanisms for biowarfare agents, which are clearly illegal under the BWC and its domestic implementing legislation. Please clarify and explain.

29) We sought and received some clarification from the DoD[3] as to whether the FPEIS reference (paragraph 1.2.2.1) to revision of the mission of the CBDP in 2003 was the result of the President's adoption of the new National Security Directives of September 2002 and December 2002. Please explain.

Article I of the Bioweapons Convention ("BWC") obligates the state contracting parties as follows:

> [N]ever in any circumstances to develop, produce, stockpile or otherwise acquire or retain:
>
> Microbial or other biological agents, or toxins whatever their origin or method of production, of types and in quantities that have no justification for prophylactic, protective or other peaceful purposes;
>
> Weapons, equipment or means of delivery designed to use such agents or toxins for hostile purposes or in armed conflict.

Despite popular misconceptions to the contrary which are evidently shared by the DoD, Article I of the Bioweapons Convention does not create an exception for "defense" or "deterrence", let alone "retaliation", but only for "prophylactic, protective or other peaceful purposes". Those who drafted and adopted the BWC were only too aware that "defense" is not necessarily "peaceful". The U.S. government appears to be violating the general rule of bioweapons prohibition found in Article I, and as well, the domestic statutory prohibitions.[4] The FPEIS does not discuss or certify whether the CBDP is in compliance with these provisions of law, which it is obligated to do. Please clarify and explain.

In Working Paper BWC/CONF.V/COW/WP.17 submitted by the United States to the Fifth Review Conference of the BWC, dated November 26, 2001, *i.e.,* right after the terrorist anthrax attacks on the U.S. Congress, the Bush Administration officially took the position that the BWC's complaint and investigation procedures applied to allegations concerning both the use and the threat of use of biological or toxin weapons:

"The States Parties reaffirm their agreement to consult, at the request of any State Party, regarding allegations of use or threat of use of bacteriological (biological) or toxin weapons and to cooperate fully with the United Nations Secretary-General in carrying out such investigations." However, the Administration's National Strategy Directives of September 2002 and December 2002, conjoined with the Pentagon's FPEIS/CBDP of May 2004, have overridden that commitment and appear to comprise a plan to threaten the world community with the criminal first use of biological weapons.

Since December 2002, the U.S. government has had in place an official policy providing the framework to initiate, fight and "win" a war of aggression by means of nuclear, biological, and chemical (NBC) weapons of mass destruction (WMD). There has been no public debate anywhere on this new official preparedness to exercise unprecedented aggressive intent and possible action as American foreign policy. The U.S. appears to have dedicated itself to preparedness for waging a first-strike chemical and bioweaponry war. Please clarify and explain.

The picture that emerges from the details missing from the FPEIS, taken together with those details which have been disclosed in the NEPA documents, and analyzed against the 2002-2003 sea changes in national defense policy, compels supplementation of the FPEIS. We request that supplementation take place immediately, and that approval of the FPEIS be waylaid indefinitely in the interests of spurring the missing public debate.

NEPA supplies the needed process for such scrutiny and discussion. NEPA declares a national policy of protecting and promoting environmental quality. *See* 42 U.S.C. § 4321, 4331(a); *Robertson v. Methow Valley Citizens Council*, 490 U.S. 332, 348 (1989). To implement this policy, NEPA requires federal agencies to follow certain procedures before undertaking projects that will affect the environment. Thus, although NEPA establishes environmental quality as a substantive goal, it is well settled that NEPA does not mandate that agencies reach particular substantive results. Instead, it simply sets forth procedures that agencies must follow. *Robertson*, 490 U.S. at 350; *Vermont Yankee Nuclear Power Corp. v. Natural Resources Defense Council, Inc.*, 435 U.S. 519, 558 (1978). In other words, "[i]f the adverse environmental effects of . . . proposed action[s] are adequately identified and evaluated, [agencies are] not constrained by NEPA from deciding that other values outweigh the environmental costs." *Robertson*, 490 U.S. at 350.

Central to NEPA's procedural focus is the requirement that federal agencies prepare EISs to be included "in every recommendation or report on proposals for . . . major Federal actions significantly affecting the quality of the human environment." 42 U.S.C. § 4332(2)(C). Preparation of an EIS serves the national policy of protecting and promoting environmental quality in two ways. First, it ensures that an agency, when deciding whether to approve a project, will carefully consider, or take a "hard look" at, the project's environmental effects. *Robertson*, 490 U.S. at 349 . Second, it ensures that relevant information about a proposed project will be made available to members of the public so that they may play a role in both the decision-making process and the implementation of the decision. *Id.*

But the preparation of an EIS does not complete an agency's NEPA duties. NEPA requires agencies to take a "hard look" at the environmental consequences of their proposed projects even *after* an EIS has been prepared. *Marsh v. Oregon Natural Resources Council,* 490 U.S. 360, 374 (1989). An agency must prepare a supplemental EIS when "[t]here are significant new circumstances or information relevant to environmental concerns and bearing on the proposed action or its impacts." 40 C.F.R. ' 1502.9(c)(1)(ii)." "'[T]he new circumstance must present a *seriously* different picture of the environmental impact of the proposed project from what was previously envisioned.'" *Hickory Neighborhood Defense League v. Skinner,* 893 F.2d 58, 63 (4th Cir. 1990) (quoting *Sierra Club v. Froehlke,* 816 F.2d 205, 210 (5th Cir. 1987)).

We submit that the law requires serious reconsideration of the current FPEIS. This is necessary in order for the

Department of Defense to address and enable the goals of democratic participation which are inherent under NEPA. The public's comment opportunity must be a meaningful one. *See American Med. Ass'n v. Reno*, 57 F.3d 1129, 1132-33 (D.C. Cir. 1995); *Engine Mfrs. Ass'n v. EPA*, 20 F.3d 1177, 1181 (D.C. Cir. 1994); *Connecticut Light & Power Co. v. Nuclear Regulatory Comm'n*, 673 F.2d 525, 530 (D.C. Cir. 1982) ("To allow an agency to play hunt the peanut with technical information, hiding or disguising the information that it employs, is to condone a practice in which the agency treats what should be a genuine interchange as mere bureaucratic sport"); *MCI Telecomms. Corp. v. FCC*, 57 F.3d 1136, 1141, 1142 (D.C. Cir. 1995) ("An agency may not turn the provision of notice into a bureaucratic game of hide and seek").

We respectfully ask that you consider and respond to our comments, and that the Department of Defense supplement the FPEIS prior to taking any record of decision. We look forward to hearing from you at your earliest convenience.

Thank you very much.

Very truly yours,

/s/ Francis A. Boyle (with permission)
Francis A. Boyle, Esq.

/s/ Terry J. Lodge
Terry J. Lodge, Esq.

cc (via email): JoLane D. Souris <jolane.souris@us.army.mil>

---

[1]   1.2.2.1 Mission Objectives and Program Management
Prior to 2003, the mission of the DoD CBDP was to provide world-class CB defense capabilities to allow U.S. military forces to survive and successfully complete their operational missions in battlespace environments contaminated with CBW agents. In 2003, however, this mission expanded to cover military capability to operate in the face of threats in homeland security missions, *as well as warfighter missions.* . . . [Emphasis added.]

2   50 USCS § 1512 (2005), § 1512: Transportation, open air testing, and disposal; Presidential determination; report to Congress; notice to Congress and State Governors None of the funds authorized to be appropriated by this Act or any other Act may be used for the transportation of any lethal chemical or any biological warfare agent to or from any military installation in the United States, the open air testing of any such agent within the United States, or the disposal of any such agent within the United States until the following procedures have been implemented: (1) the Secretary of Defense (hereafter referred to in this section [50 USCS §§ 1511-1515, 1517] as the "Secretary") has determined that the transportation or testing proposed to be made is necessary in the interests of national security; (2) the Secretary has brought the particulars of the proposed transportation, testing, or disposal to the attention of the Secretary of Health, Education, and Welfare [Secretary of Health and Human Services], who in turn may direct the Surgeon General of the Public Health Service and other qualified persons to review such particulars with respect to any hazards to public health and safety which such transportation, testing, or disposal may pose and to recommend what precautionary measures are necessary to protect the public health and safety; (3) the Secretary has implemented any precautionary measures recommended in accordance with paragraph (2) above (including, where practicable, the detoxification of any such agent, if such agent is to be transported to or from a military installation for disposal): Provided, however, That in the event the Secretary finds the recommendation submitted by the Surgeon General would have the effect of preventing the proposed transportation, testing, or disposal, the President may determine that overriding considerations of national security require such transportation, testing, or disposal be conducted. Any transportation, testing, or disposal conducted pursuant to such a Presidential determination shall be carried out in the safest practicable manner, and the President shall report his determination and an explanation thereof to the President of the Senate and the Speaker of the House of Representatives as far in advance as practicable; and (4) the Secretary has provided notification that the transportation, testing, or disposal will take place, except where a Presidential determination has been made: (A) to the President of the Senate and the Speaker of the House of Representatives at least 10 days before any such transportation or disposal will be commenced and at least 30 days before any such testing or disposal will be commenced; (B) to the Governor of any State through which such agents will be transported, such notification to be provided appropriately in advance of any such transportation.

3   Professor Boyle contacted Ms. JoLane Souris, Environmental Coordinator, U.S. Army Medical Research and Material Command,

at Fort Detrick, Maryland, designated in the *Federal Register* (Vol. 68 No. 86, May 5, 2003, at page 23705) as the Pentagon's designated information contact person for the then-Draft Programmatic Environment Impact Statement for the CBDP. He asked her if the 2003 revision of the CBDP was a result of the Pentagon implementing the Bush Jr. September 2002 and December 2002 national strategy directives discussed above. She responded that this was "probably" the case. Reproduced below is a copy of this email correspondence:

From: Boyle, Francis [mailto: FBOYLE@LAW.UIUC.EDU]
Sent: Tuesday, May 03, 2005 4:23 PM
TO: Boyle, Francis; Souris, JoLane D Ms USAMRMC
Subject: Question?

Hi: I am going through the FPEIS for the CBDP and have a question. paragraph 1.2.2.1 states that the mission of the CBDP was revised in 2003. I was wondering if that revision was the result of the President"s adoption of the new National Security Directives of September 2002 and December 2002?
Thanks.
fab.
Francis A. Boyle
From: Souris, JoLane D Ms USAMRMC
[jolane.souris@us.army.mi]
Sent: Wednesday, May 04, 2005 2:23 PM
To: fboyle@law.uiuc.edu
Subject: FW: Question?
Follow Up Flag: Follow up
Flag Status: Flagged

Mr. Boyle,
I did some research on this but have no definitive answer. The CBDP Overview where this came from merely stated the new mission statement. I would think that the National Security Directives probably did play in that change.

JoLane
JoLane Souris, CHMM
USAMRMC Environmental Manager
MCMR-ZC-S
504 Scott Street
Fort Detrick, MD 21702-5012
301-619-2004
DSN 343-2004
Fax 301-619-6627

In follow-up email correspondence to Professor Boyle on May 4, 2005 at 2:48 p.m., Ms. Souris stated that this assessment was in part based upon "the information just told to us in interviews". I asked Ms. Souris to provide me with any documentation on this matter, which she kindly agreed to look into. On May 12, 2005, she informed me that she had no more information to report about my inquiry.

4 18 U.S.C. § 175 (2004): (a) In general. Whoever knowingly develops, produces, stockpiles, transfers, acquires, retains, or possesses any biological agent, toxin, or delivery system for use as a weapon, or knowingly assists a foreign state or any organization to do so, or attempts, threatens, or conspires to do the same, shall be fined under this title or imprisoned for life or any term of years, or both. There is extraterritorial Federal jurisdiction over an offense under this section committed by or against a national of the United States. (b) Additional offense. Whoever knowingly possesses any biological agent, toxin, or delivery system of a type or in a quantity that, under the circumstances, is not reasonably justified by a prophylactic, protective, bona fide research, or other peaceful purpose, shall be fined under this title, imprisoned not more than 10 years, or both. In this subsection, the terms "biological agent" and "toxin" do not encompass any biological agent or toxin that is in its naturally occurring environment, if the biological agent or toxin has not been cultivated, collected, or otherwise extracted from its natural source.
(c) Definition. For purposes of this section, the term "for use as a weapon" includes the development, production, transfer, acquisition, retention, or possession of any biological agent, toxin, or delivery system for other than prophylactic, protective, bona fide research, or other peaceful purposes.
See, also, 18 U.S.C. § 229: Prohibited activities
(a) Unlawful conduct. Except as provided in subsection (b), it shall be unlawful for any person knowingly
    (1) to develop, produce, otherwise acquire, transfer directly or indirectly, receive, stockpile, retain, own, possess, or use, or threaten to use, any chemical weapon; or
    (2) to assist or induce, in any way, any person to violate paragraph (1), or to attempt to conspire to violate paragraph (1).
(b) Exempted agencies and persons. —
    (1) In general. Subsection (a) does not apply to the retention, ownership, possession, transfer, or receipt of a chemical weapon by a department, agency, or other entity of the United States, or by a person described in paragraph (2), pending destruction of the weapon.

Conclusion

Since the U.S. Supreme Court's installation of George W. Bush as President in January of 2001, the peoples of the world have witnessed a government in the United States of America that demonstrates little if any respect for fundamental considerations of international law, international organizations, and human rights, let alone appreciation of the requirements for maintaining international peace and security. What the world has watched instead is a comprehensive and malicious assault upon the integrity of the international legal order by a group of men and women who are thoroughly Machiavellian in their perception of international relations and in their conduct of both foreign policy and domestic affairs.

This is not simply a question of giving or withholding the benefit of the doubt when it comes to complicated matters of foreign affairs and defense policies to a U.S. government charged with the security of both its own citizens and those of its allies in Europe, the Western Hemisphere, and the Pacific. Rather, the Bush Jr. administration's foreign policies represent a gross deviation from those basic rules of international deportment and civilized behavior that the United States government had traditionally played the pioneer role in promoting for the entire world community. Even more seriously, in many instances specific components of the Bush Jr. administration's foreign policies as exercised at Guantanamo Bay, in Iraq, in Afghanistan and elsewhere, constitute ongoing criminal activity under well-recognized principles of both international law and U.S. domestic law, and in particular the Nuremberg Charter, the Nuremberg Judgment, and the Nuremberg Principles.

Depending upon the substantive issues involved, those international crimes typically include but are not limited to the Nuremberg offenses of crimes against peace, crimes against humanity, and war crimes, as well as grave breaches of the

Four Geneva Conventions of 1949 and the 1907 Hague Regulations on land warfare, systematic torture, organized enforced disappearances, and assassinations. In international legal terms, the Bush Jr. administration itself should be viewed as constituting an ongoing criminal conspiracy under both international criminal law and U.S. domestic law. These allegations are elaborated at much greater length in my 2004 work, *Destroying World Order: U.S. Imperialism in the Middle East Before and After September 11*, which offers in the final chapter, as recourse, "A Guide to the Impeachment of George W. Bush" on these grounds.

We are returned to the recourse of impeachment in specific regard to the issues raised by this book—due to the pursuit of illegal and criminal biological warfare programs by the Bush Jr. administration and its Neo-conservative operatives at the Pentagon, the C.I.A., and the Department of Homeland Security. As outlined in earlier sections of this book, these, inter alia, constitute "high Crimes and Misdemeanors" that further warrant their impeachment and removal from office under Article II, Section 4 of the United States Constitution:

> The President, Vice President and all civil Officers of the United States, shall be removed from Office on Impeachment for, and Conviction of, Treason, Bribery, or other high Crimes and Misdemeanors.

Our concern, as Americans, can surely only be deepened by our having borne witness to the disastrous criminal incapacity—and, indeed, unwillingness—of the Bush Administration to respond to the needs of the civilian population ravaged by Hurricane Katrina. Hurricane Katrina demonstrates precisely the formidable environmental dangers posed to the American people by these biowarfare labs, agents, scientists, contracts and activities promiscuously replicating all over the country. Now, in the immediate aftermath of the monumental devastation wreaked by Hurricane Katrina, can the American people truly be expected to readily accept the self-interested assurances by the already compromised Centers for Disease Control and Prevention (CDC) that there has been no loss or release of any of the numerous deadly biowarfare agents used at the five BSL Level-3 biowarfare labs in the New Orleans area.[87] Or, extrapolating from the widely demonstrated incompetence of the federal government in dealing with large-scale population relief in New Orleans, can the American people be truly certain that any federal or state Civilian Defense against biological or chemical warfare that they might purport to institute would provide effective protection for our cities and their populations, in the event either of attack or of accident—sufficient to warrant their proceeding apace with these programs, with the increased likelihood that the weapons' existence and/or possible use will give rise to responding (or even pre-emptive) attacks, or even simply disastrous accidents, on the American mainland?

We must defend ourselves against these irresponsible developments being forwarded by an administration which—simply put—does not care about the well being of the great masses of the American people, and this defense is impeachment. Our witness of the racist and class-based criminal mistreatment inflicted by the Bush Jr. administration upon the victims of Hurricane Katrina both demonstrates the need, and provides yet a further grounds for, the impeachment of President Bush Jr., Vice President Cheney, and Secretary of Homeland Security Michael Chertoff for denying Equal Protection of the Laws to the Katrina Victims because they are African Americans and because they are Poor in violation of the Fifth and Fourteenth Amendments to the United States Constitution. Let us bear in mind: in biowarfare attacks or accidents, the victims shall certainly be in mass proportions, but the casualties will not restricted by class or race.

I have already forwarded a preliminary version of this book to appropriate authorities at the Judiciary Committee of the U.S. House of Representatives for inclusion on the growing list of impeachable offenses committed by President Bush Jr. et al. You, the reader, should contact your elected Member of the U.S. House of Representatives and demand that he or she introduce our draft Bills of Impeachment as soon as possible.

The longer we delay this necessary and principled impeachment process against Bush, Jr. and his Neo-conservatives, the greater will be the disaster for all the peoples of the world and even here in the United States. Their criminal negligence and resulting mass homicides constitute "other high Crimes and Misdemeanors" within the meaning of Article II, Section 4 of the U.S. Constitution quoted above.

Despite the best efforts by the Bush Jr. Leaguers to the contrary, we American Citizens still have our First Amendment Rights: Freedom of Speech, Freedom of Association, Freedom of Assembly, Freedom to Petition our Government for the Redress of these massive Grievances, Civil Resistance, etc. We are going to have to start vigorously exercising all of our First Amendment Rights right now. We must use them or else, as the saying goes, we will lose them. We must act now for the good of the People of America as well as the Peoples of the world itself.

Notwithstanding all of the serious flaws demonstrated by successive United States governments that this author has amply documented elsewhere during the past quarter century as a Professor of Law, the truth of the matter is that the United States of America is still the oldest constitutional democracy in the world today.

We the People of the United States must fight to keep it that way!

CRITIQUE OF THE PENTAGON'S BIOLOGICAL DEFENSE RESEARCH PROGRAM (1988)

In May of 1988 the Committee (later Council) for Responsible Genetics requested that I submit to the Pentagon a critical analysis of its Draft Programmatic Environmental Impact Statement on the Department of Defense's Biological Defense Research Program, which was dated 12 May 1988. The Foundation on Economic Trends had to force this document out of the Reagan administration's Neo-conservative Pentagon by means of filing a lawsuit in U.S. federal court under the authority of the National Environmental Policy Act (NEPA) of 1969. According to the U.S. Environmental Protection Agency: "NEPA requires federal agencies to integrate environmental values into their decision making processes by considering the environmental impacts of their proposed actions and reasonable alternatives to those actions. To meet this requirement, federal agencies prepare a detailed statement known as an Environmental Impact Statement (EIS)." For reasons already explained in this book, the Reagan administration's Neo-conservative Pentagon did not want to produce that environmental impact statement (EIS) for its Biological Defense Research Program (BDRP). Hence the need for a federal lawsuit compelling the Reaganite Neo-con Pentagon to obey this federal law and come clean.

To the best of my knowledge, this Draft EIS for the BDRP was the first comprehensive analysis of its biological warfare program that had ever been produced and publicly released by the Pentagon. Not surprisingly, this Draft EIS/BDRP was a complete and total whitewash of the Pentagon's biological warfare program that contained within itself components that violated the Biological Weapons Convention, as well as whitewashing the negative environmental consequences of the BDRP. Interestingly enough, *this Pentagon whitewash of the BDRP was prepared by individuals associated with the U.S. Army's Construction Engineering Lab located on the University of Illinois at Urbana-Champaign campus—a hotbed for biowarfare work.*

In May of 2004 the Bush Jr. administration's Neo-conservative Pentagon produced the second major whitewash of its biowarfare program by means of promulgating its Final Programmatic Environmental Impact Statement (FPEIS) for the Chemical and Biological Defense Program (CBDP). For reasons already explained in this book, the Pentagon's 2004 FPEIS/CBDP tried but failed to whitewash the illegal biowarfare components of the CBDP that violate the Biological Weapons Convention and the Biological Weapons Anti-terrorism Act of 1989 as currently amended, as well as the detrimental environmental consequences of the CBDP. Most of the objections to the BDRP that were raised in my 5 August 1988 Memorandum reprinted below likewise apply to the 2004 CBDP. This is because both biowarfare programs were designed and implemented by many of the same Neo-conservative operatives who worked for both the Reagan administration and the Bush Jr. administration.

August 5, 1988
<u>Express Mail</u>

Phillip K. Russell
Major General, Medical Corps Commander
U.S. Army Medical Research and Development Command
Attention: SGRD-PA
Fort Detrick
Frederick, Maryland 21701-5012

Re: <u>Draft Programmatic Environmental Impact Statement on the Department of Defense Biological Defense Research Program (May 1988)</u>

Dear General Russell:

1. My name is Francis A. Boyle and I am a Professor of International Law at the University of Illinois in Champaign. I am also a member of the Subcommittee on the Military Uses of Biological Research

of the Committee for Responsible Genetics. In that capacity, I have been closely involved in the proposed Draft Implementing Legislation for the Biological Weapons Convention of 1972 that is currently pending in Congress. Enclosed you will find a copy of the Testimony I submitted in support thereof to the Subcommittee on Immigration, Refugees and International Law of the House Judiciary Committee, dated 23 March 1988, together with a Supplement thereto excerpted from a Memorandum I drafted on that subject dated 1 April 1987. Attached you will also find a 1986 Article I wrote on the Reagan administration's Chemical and Biological Warfare Programs that has been reprinted by the Department of the Air Force, in Current News, Special Edition No. 1586, Chemical Weapons, at 6 (28 May 1987). Finally, a copy of my resumé has also been attached for your convenience. I should make it clear, however, that I am writing here only on my own behalf as a recognized expert on the subject of international law and biological warfare.

2. Your 12 May 1988 Circular Letter invited public comment on the Draft Programmatic Environmental Impact Statement on the Department of Defense Biological Defense Research Program (BDRP) (May 1988), that will hereinafter be referred to as the DEIS. In my expert opinion, there are several aspects of the DEIS that raise serious questions as to the BDRP's compliance with the stringent terms of the 1972 Biological Weapons Convention (BWC). Therefore, I would respectfully request that you "task" someone from your Command to respond to the following comments and questions I have posed on this matter. A prompt, forthright, and honest response to these questions will go a long way toward alleviating the concerns held by me and many other members of the Committee for Responsible Genetics about the BDRP.

3. For example, right at the very outset of the DEIS, section 1.1 directly raises the issue of BDRP compliance with the BWC in the following words: "The Department of Defense (DOD) cannot ignore completely the possibility that BW threats exist and fail to provide any deterrents to their potential application, much less fail to provide a reasonable level of protection to U.S. forces." (Emphasis added.) (page 1.1). Section 1-1 clearly raises the question of whether or not the BDRP has for its purpose the development of offensive BW threats to serve as "deterrents" to an alleged or

!10

supposed threat by an adversary of the United States. Moreover, section 1.1 makes it quite clear that the development of such "deterrents" is a DOD objective that is quite different from providing "a reasonable level of protection to U.S. forces." Clearly, "protection" is permissible under the terms of the Biological Weapons Convention. But since the DEIS distinguishes "protection" from "deterrents," then obviously the DOD intends to mean that such "deterrents" are something beyond mere "protection." If so, then there exists a distinct possibility that DOD research, development and testing of such "deterrents" would violate the BWC.

4. For example, in the areas of chemical weapons, nuclear weapons, and conventional weapons, whenever the Department of Defense has talked about developing "deterrents" to their respective uses, it has always meant the research, development, testing and deployment of chemical, nuclear, and conventional weapons that will be used in retaliation in the event an adversary should resort to the first use of such weapons. Likewise, the entirety of the DEIS produces the strong implication that the Department of Defense is seriously contemplating the development of biological weapons in order to serve as "deterrents" to their expected use by an adversary of the United States government. In any event, a reasonable person reading the DEIS could certainly conclude that the Department of Defense is moving toward the development of BW "deterrents" that would be illegal under the terms of the BWC. At the very least, I suspect that is how the Soviet Union will read the DEIS. <u>What concrete assurances can the DOD provide to the American people and to the Soviet government that this is not the case?</u>

5. Next, DEIS section 2.1 cites the Sverdlovsk incident and allegations of the use of toxins in Southeast Asia and Afghanistan by the Soviet Union as evidence of a resurgence of interest in biological warfare agents by the supposed adversaries of the United States government. Yet all of the scholarly literature written on these subjects agrees on the points that "yellow rain" was nothing more than bee feces and that the Sverdlovsk incident was produced by contaminated cattle feed.[88] Since these matters are discussed at greater length in my 1986 <u>Article</u> and in the recent book by Piller and Yamamoto entitled <u>Gene Wars</u> (1988), I will not bother to review that literature in detail here. Suffice it to say that the Department of Defense can not produce a realistic

assessment of the alleged biological weapons threat to the United States of America when its only two unclassified pieces of evidence have been definitively proven to be erroneous. <u>How can the American public rely upon the integrity of the DEIS when it is premised upon such faulty assumptions?</u>

6. The entire DEIS itself has been seriously compromised by dredging up such unsubstantiated and spurious allegations that have now been completely discredited by the scientific community. Whoever on your Staff was responsible for drafting these sections of the DEIS did no good service to the Department of Defense in reproducing such disingenuous allegations here. The DEIS's reliance upon these thoroughly debunked allegations simply raises the question of whether the Department of Defense is purposefully creating the specter of a Soviet offensive BW threat in order to justify its own development of retaliatory/offensive BW "deterrents" (to use the DOD's own term) under the guise of the BDRP.

7. For example, the DEIS lists my institution, the University of Illinois at Urbana-Champaign, as a secondary research site for the BDRP. I inquired from your Command as to the nature of four contracts that have been let out by the DOD to researchers at the University of Illinois as part of the BDRP. To my surprise, I discovered that two of these contracts (viz., DAMD 1782C2179 and DAMD 1785C5224) relate to tricothecene mycotoxins, which are said to be the active ingredients of so-called "yellow rain." Yet, since it has already been established that "yellow rain" is nothing more than bee feces, there is absolutely no legitimate reason whatsoever for these researchers to be engaged in toxicological studies related to tricothecene mycotoxins for the DOD. At the very least, it seems to me that this weapons-specific research is what the DOD likes to call "dual-use": that is, it generates results that can be put to both offensive and defensive purposes depending upon the mere intention of the researchers involved or of the DOD. The fact that there has never been an offensive "yellow rain" threat to the United States indicates to me that perhaps the purpose of such "yellow rain" research is to generate results that can be put to prohibited uses. <u>What concrete assurances can the DOD provide to the American people and to the University of Illinois community that such is not the case beyond DOD's own self-interested disclaimers?</u>

8. Furthermore, it appears from the public description of the DOD studies at the University of Illinois that mycotoxins and bluegreen-algae toxin are being injected into pigs (viz., DAMD 1785C5224 and DAMD 1785C5241). Nevertheless, DEIS Appendix 3 lists the University of Illinois as a secondary site that falls into Risk Category VII, which is defined as "Other Program Research and Activities*," a term that is further defined as "*Includes either very low risk or non-risk activities which do not fit into the above [I-VI] categories." (page A3-1) Quite frankly, I find it completely misleading to say that the injection of pigs with mycotoxins and bluegreen-algae toxin are "very low risk or non-risk activities" that only require the lowest degree of minimal protections according to BDRP procedures. The DEIS's obfuscation of the weapons-specific type of research that is really going on at the University of Illinois, together with the misleading description of such research as being low-risk or non-risk, call into question the entire categorization scheme for all of the contracts at the so-called secondary sites in the BDRP. This section of the DEIS must be substantially revised and significantly more information on the exact nature of BDRP contracts and secondary site protections must be disclosed to the people inhabiting the nearby vicinities.

9. DEIS section 2.4.1 states with respect to gene cloning of protein toxins: "The general approach is to identify the portions of the protein toxin responsible for eliciting immunity, as opposed to that portion of the molecule responsible for toxicity." (Emphasis added.) (page 2-5). The use of the words "general approach" implies that there are also "other approaches" undertaken by the DOD with respect to this particular type of research. More concretely, there is nothing to prevent researchers from cloning the portion of the molecule responsible for toxicity, which they have already implicitly identified when distinguishing it from the immunogenic portion. The DEIS provides absolutely no assurance or mechanism to guarantee that this is not occurring under the aegis of the BDRP even though the DEIS makes it quite clear that such prohibited research can in fact occur.

10. In this regard, the various federal laws, statutes and regulations mentioned in the DEIS are completely inadequate to implement the strict terms of the Biological Weapons Convention for the reasons explained in my 1988 Testimony and in my 1987

Memorandum that I prepared on behalf of the Committee for Responsible Genetics, copies of which are attached to this letter. Nowhere in the DEIS has your Staff indicated that qualified and independent legal experts have vetted the BDRP in accordance with the strict terms of the BWC, or that such oversight and examination would be conscientious, continuous and comprehensive. What assurances do the American people have that the Department of Defense is scrupulously adhering to the terms of the Biological Weapons Convention other than the self-exculpating DEIS statements to that effect?

11. I would submit that if the Department of Defense wants to obtain public acceptance and support for the BDRP, then it must establish both external and internal procedures whereby independent lawyers, in addition to independent scientific experts, can guarantee and assure to the American people that the BWC is being strictly adhered to throughout all aspects of the BDRP. Since the BDRP is generally not classified, such procedures should not be too difficult to set up, assuming the DOD really wants to. I would be happy to meet with you and your Staff in order to establish such procedures that might provide some degree of credibility with respect to BDRP/BWC compliance in the eyes of the American scientific and legal communities.

12. DEIS section 4.2.2 states that it "would not be appropriate, even if it could be done institutionally, to transfer defense responsibility to another agency or organization." (page 4-6). Yet that is precisely what has historically been done with respect to nuclear weapons. Originally, the Truman administration decided to establish civilian control, as opposed to military control, over nuclear weapons by means of creating the Atomic Energy Commission. Such governmental supervision over nuclear weapons now resides in the civilian Department of Energy, which is exclusively responsible for the research, design, development and testing of nuclear weapons systems themselves, not the Department of Defense. The same type of civilian function could certainly be performed with respect to the BDRP by the National Institutes of Health, for example. In any event, the DEIS dismissed this alternative out of hand without even bothering to discuss or analyze it. A revised DEIS must contain a detailed analysis of the utility of this civilian alternative by your Staff.

13. Indeed, DEIS Executive Summary section ES.7 dismissed three options for the BDRP out of hand without even bothering to comment upon them: the elimination of aerosol testing; placing a moratorium on research involving genetic-engineered micro-organisms (GEMs); and transferring the management responsibility for the BDRP to a non-military agency. (page ES-4) Whoever was responsible for preparing the DEIS was grossly negligent in not producing a comprehensive analysis as to why either one if not all three of these alternatives should have been seriously considered with respect to all or significant parts of the BDRP. I would respectfully request that you go back to your Staff and demand that they produce a revised DEIS that seriously addresses these three aspects of the problem.

14. Proceeding sequentially through the DEIS, I next have serious concerns with respect to BDRP research going on at secondary sites outside the territorial jurisdiction of the United States. I would like to know whether or not and how the Department of Defense is making sure that such research is being conducted in accordance with the strict terms of the Biological Weapons Convention irrespective of whether the host country is a party to the BWC. There is a potential for the Department of Defense to take the position that it is not responsible for absolutely guaranteeing that BDRP research conducted in countries not parties to the BWC is consistent with the terms of the Convention. Is this the case or not?

15. For example, I am especially concerned that BDRP research is currently taking place in Liberia, which is not a party to the BWC, as indicated in Appendix 3, page A3-4. As you undoubtedly know, Liberia is ruled by a ruthless dictator named Samuel K. Doe, who is kept in power by the Central Intelligence Agency and the DOD Army's Special Forces. What assurances can you provide to the American people that BDRP research currently being conducted in Liberia is in full compliance with the terms of the BWC when Liberia is not a party to the BWC? Such questionable foreign BDRP research contracts create the strong suspicion that the Department of Defense has been purposely letting out BDRP contracts to sources in Liberia and other non-BWC states for the express purpose of circumventing or undermining the stringent controls of the BWC.

16. In this regard, I have also noted in DEIS Appendix 3 that both the Wistar Institute of Philadelphia, Pennsylvania and the Pan-American Health Organization in Argentina are classified as secondary sites for the BDRP. Since that is the case, I would like to know whether or not DOD funding under the aegis of BDRP research or otherwise was behind the controversial experiment developed by the Wistar Institute involving a genetically-engineered rabies vaccine that was injected into animals in Argentina without official sanction by the governmental authorities of that country. Argentinian officials have since charged that the virus spread beyond the animals that had been vaccinated. If DOD funding was behind that Wistar experiment, then it is obvious that DOD quality and safety controls have proven to be completely inadequate. In any event, because of the Argentinian affair, it appears that Wistar should not under any circumstances be allowed to conduct BDRP research. What assurances can you provide to the American people that comprehensive controls will be instituted with respect to all BDRP research occurring at so-called secondary sites whether in the United States or abroad by irresponsible contractors such as Wistar?

17. DEIS section 5.2.1.4 at page 5-6 admits that the BDRP is engaged in the process of identifying and counteracting so-called "potential threat agents." Yet, once again, the American people have no guarantee that the Department of Defense is using GEMs to produce a vaccine as opposed to the weapon itself. DEIS page 5-9 admits that BDRP uses of recombinant techniques are with the goal of producing "a less virulent strain." But then a fortiori, using the same recombinant techniques, the BDRP can certainly produce a "more virulent strain." What independently verifiable guarantees can the Department of Defense provide to the American people that this is not going to happen under the aegis of the BDRP?

18. DEIS Appendix 4, section 1.3 at page A4-3 provides no rationale whatsoever for the rejection of simulants as an alternative to the use of highly dangerous organisms for various aspects of the BDRP. The use of simulants for a variety of purposes is simply dismissed out of hand. This section of the DEIS is completely inadequate and slipshod. Your Staff needs to produce a revised DEIS that contains a comprehensive analysis of the potential use of simulants throughout all aspects of the BDRP.

19. DEIS Appendix 4, section 3.2 states that with respect to toxins, research, development and testing activities include: "structural analyses to identify the parts of a toxin responsible for immunity." Yet, since that is the case, then the same "structural analyses" can also be used to "identify the parts of a toxin responsible for" pathogenicity. Once again, such dual-use studies and activities raise serious questions of BDRP compliance with the BWC. What assurances can the DOD provide to the American people that these "structural analyses" are not being put to prohibited purposes? A similar criticism applies to a DOD contract here at the University of Illinois for The Development of a Toxic Knowledge System (viz., DAMD 1787C7114).

20. The above analysis contains most of the major points I wish to make on the proposed DEIS for the BDRP. I do hope that a responsible person under your Command will have the opportunity to provide a formal, written, and comprehensive response to these questions. If necessary, I will be happy to meet with someone from your Command in order to discuss these concerns. However, unless and until I receive an adequate response to these points and questions in writing, I will remain opposed to the BDRP. In addition, I will also recommend that the Committee for Responsible Genetics use its considerable influence and prestige within the scientific community and elsewhere to actively oppose the BDRP by all means possible. Finally, I will also have to make a similar recommendation to those lawyers' organizations of which I am a member.

I look forward to hearing from you at your earliest convenience. And thank you very much for your kind attention to this matter.

Yours very truly,

Francis A. Boyle
Professor of Law
encl's.
cc: The Committee for Responsible Genetics

BIOWARFARE RESEARCH AT THE UNIVERSITY OF ILLINOIS COLLEGE OF VETERINARY MEDICINE

August 24, 1988

William C. Wagner
Professor and Head
University of Illinois
Department of Veterinary Biosciences
3516 Veterinary Medicine Basic Sciences Building
2001 South Lincoln Avenue
Urbana, Illinois 61801

Dear Professor Wagner:

Thank you very much for your kind letter of August 22. It was most appreciated. I read it with a good deal of interest. After I sent the August 5, 1988 letter on the Biological Defense Research Program (BDRP) to the Director of the U.S. Army Medical Research and Development Command, I requested computer printouts for the Department of Defense's own descriptions of their BDRP contracts with the University of Illinois, copies of which are available in my office for your inspection. They make for quite interesting reading.

The computer printout of the contract with V. L. Beasley on Pathophysiology and Toxicokinetic Studies of Blue-Green Algae in the Swine Model is clearly listed therein as a biological warfare (BW) project. Also the contract with Harold Trammel on Development of a Toxic Knowledge System is clearly listed therein as a biological warfare project. The contract with William B. Buck on <u>Diagnosis</u> <u>and Management of Tricothecene Toxicosis in the Swine Model</u> is clearly listed therein as a biological warfare project. An earlier contract with the same Mr. Buck entitled <u>Toxicological and Analytical</u> <u>Studies with T-2 and Related Tricothecene Mycotoxins</u> is not listed as a biological warfare project. Nevertheless, the earlier contract covered the period 1 July 1982 to 30 June 1985, while the later BW contract covered the period 1 July 1985 to 31 January 1988. Hence, the later BW contract appears to be a continuation of and renewal for the earlier research contract. And since the later contract is clearly designed as a biological warfare project, then <u>a fortiori</u> the same can probably be said for the earlier research contract.

Thus, according to the Department of Defense's own records, your people are engaged in at least four biological warfare projects here on campus that I know of. Why else would DOD be funding this research? For reasons better explained in my August 5 letter, such research appears to violate the terms of the Biological Weapons Convention to which the United States government is a party. As far as I am concerned, this apparently illegal research has no role to play on a university campus and should be discontinued immediately.

If you would like, I would be more than happy to meet with you to discuss the four contracts. However, in light of the confirmation that I have received from the Department of Defense that these contracts are indeed for biological warfare purposes and unless these designations can be explained to my satisfaction, I see no alternative but to disclose this information to the members of the university community so that they can make up their own minds as to whether BW research should be conducted on campus.[89] I look forward to hearing from you at your earliest convenience.

Yours very truly,

Francis A. Boyle
Professor of Law
FAB/bw
Encl.
cc: Dean Richard Dierks
     Dean Judith Liebman
     Chancellor Morton Weir
     Professor Eric Jakobsson

PROTOCOL FOR THE PROHIBITION OF THE USE IN WAR OF ASPHYXIATING, POISONOUS OR OTHER GASES, AND OF BACTERIOLOGICAL METHODS OF WARFARE

Opened for signature: 17 June 1925; entered into force, 8 February 1928, 94 L.N.T.S. 65; 26 U.S.T.S. 571, T.I.A.S. 8061.

The undersigned Plenipotentiaries, in the name of their respective governments:

Whereas the use in war of asphyxiating, poisonous or other gases, and of all analogous liquids, materials or devices, has been justly condemned by the general opinion of the civilised world; and

Whereas the prohibition of such use has been declared in Treaties to which the majority of Powers of the world are Parties; and

To the end that this prohibition shall be universally accepted as a part of International Law, binding alike the conscience and the practice of nations;

Declare:

That the High Contracting Parties, so far as they are not already Parties to Treaties prohibiting such use, accept this prohibition, agree to extend this prohibition to the use of bacteriological methods of warfare and agree to be bound as between themselves according to the terms of this declaration.

The High Contracting Parties will exert every effort to induce other States to accede to the present Protocol. Such accession will be notified to the Government of the French Republic, and by the latter to all signatories and acceding Powers, and will take effect on the date of the notification by the Government of the French Republic.

The present Protocol, of which the English and French texts are both authentic, shall be ratified as soon as possible. It shall bear today's date.

The ratifications of the present Protocol shall be addressed to the Government of the French Republic, which will at once notify the deposit of such ratification to each of the signatory and acceding Powers.

The instruments of ratification of and accession to the present Protocol will remain deposited in the archives of the Government of the French Republic.

The present Protocol will come into force for each signatory Power as from the date of deposit of its ratification, and, from that moment, each Power will be bound as regards other Powers which have already deposited their ratifications.

In witness whereof the Plenipotentiaries have signed the present Protocol.

Done at Geneva in a single copy, the seventeenth day of June, One Thousand Nine Hundred and Twenty-Five.

Convention on the Prohibition of the Development, Production and Stockpiling of Bacteriological (Biological) and Toxin Weapons and on Their Destruction

Signed at Washington, London, and Moscow April 10, 1972
Ratification advised by U.S. Senate December 16, 1974
Ratified by U.S. President January 22, 1975
U.S. ratification deposited at Washington, London, and Moscow
March 26, 1975
Proclaimed by U.S. President March 26, 1975
Entered into force March 26, 1975

The States Parties to this Convention,

Determined to act with a view to achieving effective progress towards general and complete disarmament, including the prohibition and elimination of all types of weapons of mass destruction, and convinced that the prohibition of the development, production and stockpiling of chemical and bacteriological (biological) weapons and their elimination, through effective measures, will facilitate the achievement of general and complete disarmament under strict and effective international control,

Recognizing the important significance of the Protocol for the Prohibition of the Use in War of Asphyxiating, Poisonous or

Other Gases, and of Bacteriological Methods of Warfare, signed at Geneva on June 17, 1925, and conscious also of the contribution which the said Protocol has already made, and continues to make, to mitigating the horrors of war,

Reaffirming their adherence to the principles and objectives of that Protocol and calling upon all States to comply strictly with them,

Recalling that the General Assembly of the United Nations has repeatedly condemned all actions contrary to the principles and objectives of the Geneva Protocol of June 17, 1925,

Desiring to contribute to the strengthening of confidence between peoples and the general improvement of the international atmosphere,

Desiring also to contribute to the realization of the purposes and principles of the Charter of the United Nations,

Convinced of the importance and urgency of eliminating from the arsenals of States, through effective measures, such dangerous weapons of mass destruction as those using chemical or bacteriological (biological) agents,

Recognizing that an agreement on the prohibition of bacteriological (biological) and toxin weapons represents a first possible step towards the achievement of agreement on effective measures also for the prohibition of the development, production and stockpiling of chemical weapons, and determined to continue negotiations to that end,

Determined, for the sake of all mankind, to exclude completely the possibility of bacteriological (biological) agents and toxins being used as weapons,

Convinced that such use would be repugnant to the conscience of mankind and that no effort should be spared to minimize this risk,

Have agreed as follows:

Article I

Each State Party to this Convention undertakes never in any circumstances to develop, produce, stockpile or otherwise acquire or retain:

(1) Microbial or other biological agents, or toxins whatever their origin or method of production, of types and in quantities that have no justification for prophylactic, protective or other peaceful purposes;

(2) Weapons, equipment or means of delivery designed to use such agents or toxins for hostile purposes or in armed conflict.

Article II

Each State Party to this Convention undertakes to destroy, or to divert to peaceful purposes, as soon as possible but not later than nine months after the entry into force of the Convention, all agents, toxins, weapons, equipment and means of delivery specified in article I of the Convention, which are in its possession or under its jurisdiction or control. In implementing the provisions of this article all necessary safety precautions shall be observed to protect populations and the environment.

Article III

Each State Party to this Convention undertakes not to transfer to any recipient whatsoever, directly or indirectly, and not in any way to assist, encourage, or induce any State, group of States or international organizations to manufacture or otherwise acquire any of the agents, toxins, weapons, equipment or means of delivery specified in article I of the Convention.

Article IV

Each State Party to this Convention shall, in accordance with its constitutional processes, take any necessary measures to prohibit and prevent the development, production, stockpiling, acquisition, or retention of the agents, toxins, weapons, equipment and means of delivery specified in article I of the Convention, within the territory of such State, under its jurisdiction or under its control anywhere.

Article V

The States Parties to this Convention undertake to consult one another and to cooperate in solving any problems which may arise in relation to the objective of, or in the application of the provisions of, the Convention. Consultation and cooperation pursuant to this article may also be undertaken through appropriate international procedures within the framework of the United Nations and in accordance with its Charter.

Article VI

(1) Any State Party to this Convention which finds that any other State Party is acting in breach of obligations deriving from the provisions of the Convention may lodge a complaint with the Security Council of the United Nations. Such a complaint should include all possible evidence confirming its validity, as well as a request for its consideration by the Security Council.

(2) Each State Party to this Convention undertakes to cooperate in carrying out any investigation which the Security Council may initiate, in accordance with the provisions of the Charter of the United Nations, on the basis of the complaint received by the Council. The Security Council shall inform the States Parties to the Convention of the results of the investigation.

Article VII

Each State Party to this Convention undertakes to provide or support assistance, in accordance with the United Nations Charter, to any Party to the Convention which so requests, if the Security Council decides that such Party has been exposed to danger as a result of violation of the Convention.

Article VIII

Nothing in this Convention shall be interpreted as in any way limiting or detracting from the obligations assumed by any State under the Protocol for the Prohibition of the Use in War of Asphyxiating, Poisonous or Other Gases, and of Bacteriological Methods of Warfare, signed at Geneva on June 17, 1925.

Article IX

Each State Party to this Convention affirms the recognized objective of effective prohibition of chemical weapons and, to this end, undertakes to continue negotiations in good faith with a view to reaching early agreement on effective measures for the prohibition of their development, production and stockpiling and for their destruction, and on appropriate measures concerning equipment and means of delivery specifically designed for the production or use of chemical agents for weapons purposes.

Article X

(1) The States Parties to this Convention undertake to facilitate, and have the right to participate in, the fullest possible exchange of equipment, materials and scientific and technological information for the use of bacteriological (biological) agents and toxins for peaceful purposes. Parties to the Convention in a position to do so shall also cooperate in contributing individually or together with other States or international organizations to the further development and application of scientific discoveries in the field of bacteriology (biology) for prevention of disease, or for other peaceful purposes.

(2) This Convention shall be implemented in a manner designed to avoid hampering the economic or technological development of States Parties to the Convention or international cooperation in the field of peaceful bacteriological (biological) activities, including the international exchange of bacteriological (biological) agents and toxins and equipment for the processing, use or production of bacteriological (biological) agents and toxins for peaceful purposes in accordance with the provisions of the Convention.

Article XI

Any State Party may propose amendments to this Convention. Amendments shall enter into force for each State Party accepting the amendments upon their acceptance by a majority of the States Parties to the Convention and thereafter for each remaining State Party on the date of acceptance by it.

Article XII

Five years after the entry into force of this Convention, or earlier if it is requested by a majority of Parties to the Convention by submitting a proposal to this effect to the Depositary Governments, a conference of States Parties to the Convention shall be held at Geneva, Switzerland, to review the operation of the Convention, with a view to assuring that the purposes of the preamble and the provisions of the Convention, including the provisions concerning negotiations on chemical weapons, are being realized. Such review shall take into account any new scientific and technological developments relevant to the Convention.

Article XIII

(1) This Convention shall be of unlimited duration.

(2) Each State Party to this Convention shall in exercising its national sovereignty have the right to withdraw from the Convention if it decides that extraordinary events, related to the subject matter of the Convention, have jeopardized the supreme interests of its country. It shall give notice of such withdrawal to all other States Parties to the Convention and to the United Nations Security Council three months in advance. Such notice shall include a statement of the extraordinary events it regards as having jeopardized its supreme interests.

Article XIV

(1) This Convention shall be open to all States for signature. Any State which does not sign the Convention before its entry into force in accordance with paragraph (3) of this Article may accede to it at any time.

(2) This Convention shall be subject to ratification by signatory States. Instruments of ratification and instruments of accession shall be deposited with the Governments of the United States of America, the United Kingdom of Great Britain and Northern Ireland and the Union of Soviet Socialist Republics, which are hereby designated the Depositary Governments.

(3) This Convention shall enter into force after the deposit of instruments of ratification by twenty-two Governments, including the Governments designated as Depositaries of the Convention.

(4) For States whose instruments of ratification or accession are deposited subsequent to the entry into force of this Convention, it shall enter into force on the date of the deposit of their instruments of ratification or accession.

(5) The Depositary Governments shall promptly inform all signatory and acceding States of the date of each signature, the date of deposit of each instrument of ratification or of accession and the date of the entry into force of this Convention, and of the receipt of other notices.

(6) This Convention shall be registered by the Depositary Governments pursuant to Article 102 of the Charter of the United Nations.

Article XV

This Convention, the English, Russian, French, Spanish and Chinese texts of which are equally authentic, shall be deposited in the archives of the Depositary Governments. Duly certified copies of the Convention shall be transmitted by the Depositary Governments to the Governments of the signatory and acceding states.

IN WITNESS WHEREOF the undersigned, duly authorized, have signed this Convention.

DONE in triplicate, at the cities of Washington, London and Moscow, this tenth day of April, one thousand nine hundred and seventy-two.

ENDNOTES

FOREWORD

[1] Jonathan King & Harlee Strauss, *The Hazards of Defensive Biological Warfare Programs, in* PREVENTING A BIOLOGICAL ARMS RACE 120 (Susan Wright ed., 1990).

[2] Timothy D. Read et al., *Comparative Genome Sequencing for Discovering of Novel Polymorphisms in* Bacillus anthracis, 296 SCIENCE 2028 (2002).

BIOWARFARE AND TERRORISM

[1] *See generally* COMM. ON RESEARCH STANDARDS & PRACTICES TO PREVENT THE DESTRUCTIVE APPLICATION OF BIOTECHNOLOGY, NAT'L ACAD. OF SCIS., BIOTECHNOLOGY RESEARCH IN AN AGE OF TERRORISM 20–21 (2004); CHARLES PILLER & KEITH R. YAMAMOTO, GENE WARS: MILITARY CONTROL OVER THE NEW GENETIC TECHNOLOGIES ch. 2 (1988); George W. Christopher et al., *Biological Warfare: A Historical Perspective, in* BIOLOGICAL WEAPONS: LIMITING THE THREAT 17 (Joshua S. Lederberg ed., 1999); Susan Wright, *Evolution of Biological Warfare Policy, 1945–1990, in* PREVENTING A BIOLOGICAL ARMS RACE 26 (Susan Wright ed., 1990).

[2] Treaty on the Non-proliferation of Nuclear Weapons, July 1, 1968, 21 U.S.T. 483, 729 U.N.T.S. 161, *available at* http://disarmament.un.org/wmd/npt/ [hereinafter NPT].

[3] Convention on the Prohibition of the Development, Production, Stockpiling and Use of Chemical Weapons and on Their Destruction (Chemical Weapons Convention), Jan. 13, 1993, 1974 U.N.T.S. 45, 32 I.L.M. 800, *available at* http://disarmament.un.org/wmd/cwc/ [hereinafter CWC].

[4] On Nov. 25, 1969, Nixon directed the Department of Defense to dispose of all existing stocks of biological agents and weapons; the order was extended to include toxin agents in Feb. 1970. Robert P. Kadlec et al., *Biological Weapons Control: Prospects and Implications for the Future, in* BIOLOGICAL WEAPONS: LIMITING THE THREAT 95, 98–99 (Joshua Lederberg ed., 1999). Destruction of the U.S. biological arsenal, under the aegis of the federal Departments of Agriculture and HEW and the Ark., Colo., and Md. natural resources departments, was reportedly completed between May 1971 and Feb. 1973, although small quantities of pathogens continued to be maintained at USAMRIID at Ft. Detrick, Md. George W. Christopher et al., *Biological Warfare: A Historical Perspective, in* BIOLOGICAL WEAPONS: LIMITING THE THREAT 17, 29 (Joshua S. Lederberg ed., 1999).

5   JUDITH MILLER ET AL., GERMS: BIOLOGICAL WEAPONS AND AMERICA'S SECRET WAR 72–74 (2001); CHARLES PILLER & KEITH R. YAMAMOTO, GENE WARS: MILITARY CONTROL OVER THE NEW GENETIC TECHNOLOGIES 64 (1988); Richard Falk, *Inhibiting Reliance on Biological Weaponry: The Role and Relevance of International Law, in* PREVENTING A BIOLOGICAL ARMS RACE 241, 256 (Susan Wright ed., 1990); Gregory Koblentz, *Pathogens as Weapons: The International Security Implications of Biological Warfare*, 28 INT'L SECURITY 84, 111 (2004).

6   Convention on the Prohibition of the Development, Production and Stockpiling of Bacteriological (Biological) and Toxin Weapons and on Their Destruction (Biological and Toxin Weapons Convention), Apr. 10, 1972, 26 U.S.T. 591, 1015 U.N.T.S. 163, *available at* http://disarmament.un.org/wmd/bwc/ [hereinafter BWC].

7   CHARLES PILLER & KEITH R. YAMAMOTO, GENE WARS: MILITARY CONTROL OVER THE NEW GENETIC TECHNOLOGIES 116–20 (1988); Susan Wright & Stuart Ketcham, *The Problem of Interpreting the U.S. Biological Defense Research Program, in* PREVENTING A BIOLOGICAL ARMS RACE 169, 185–87 (Susan Wright ed., 1990).

8   *See* PEOPLE FOR THE AMERICAN WAY, THE RIGHT-WING AFFILIATIONS OF BUSH ADMINISTRATION OFFICIALS, *at* http://www.pfaw.org/pfaw/dfiles/file_145.pdf (last visited Jan. 11, 2005).

9   *See, e.g.,* Keith Rogers, *Remembering Reagan: Changes in Nuclear Arsenal Recalled,* LAS VEGAS REV., June 8, 2004, at 6A.

10   JUDITH MILLER ET AL., GERMS: BIOLOGICAL WEAPONS AND AMERICA'S SECRET WAR 83 (2001); CHARLES PILLER & KEITH R. YAMAMOTO, GENE WARS: MILITARY CONTROL OVER THE NEW GENETIC TECHNOLOGIES 154–55 (1988); Susan Wright, *Evolution of Biological Warfare Policy, 1945–1990, in* PREVENTING A BIOLOGICAL ARMS RACE 26, 48–49 (Susan Wright ed., 1990).

11   Jozef Goldblat, *The Biological Weapons Convention: An Overview,* INT'L REV. RED CROSS, May-June 1997, at 251, 254.

12   Charles Piller & Keith R. Yamamoto, *The U.S. Biological Defense Research Program in the 1980s: A Critique, in* PREVENTING A BIOLOGICAL ARMS RACE 133, 159 tbl.7.4 (Susan Wright ed., 1990).

13   COMM. ON RESEARCH STANDARDS & PRACTICES TO PREVENT THE DESTRUCTIVE APPLICATION OF BIOTECHNOLOGY, NAT'L ACAD. OF SCIS., BIOTECHNOLOGY RESEARCH IN AN AGE OF TERRORISM 23 (2004); JUDITH MILLER ET AL., GERMS: BIOLOGICAL WEAPONS AND AMERICA'S SECRET WAR 83–84 (2001); Richard Novick & Seth Shulman, *New Forms of Biological Warfare?, in* PREVENTING A BIOLOGICAL ARMS RACE 103, 104 (Susan Wright ed. 1990).

14   CHARLES PILLER & KEITH R. YAMAMOTO, GENE WARS: MILITARY CONTROL OVER THE NEW GENETIC TECHNOLOGIES 117–20 (1988); Susan Wright & Stuart Ketcham, *The Problem of Interpreting the U.S. Biological Defense Research Program, in* PREVENTING A BIOLOGICAL ARMS RACE 169, 188 (Susan Wright ed., 1990); *cf.* Raymond A. Zilinskas, *Iraq's Biological Warfare Program: The Past as Future?, in*

BIOLOGICAL WEAPONS: LIMITING THE THREAT 137, 138 (Joshua S. Lederberg ed., 1999) (major components of biological weapon are payload, munition to maintain payload virulence during delivery, delivery system, and dispersal mechanism).

15   Richard Danzig & Pamela B. Berkowsky, *Why Should We Be Concerned About Biological Warfare?, in* BIOLOGICAL WEAPONS: LIMITING THE THREAT 9, 10 (Joshua S. Lederberg ed., 1999).

16   *See generally* Charles Piller & Keith R. Yamamoto, *The U.S. Biological Defense Research Program in the 1980s: A Critique, in* PREVENTING A BIOLOGICAL ARMS RACE 133 (Susan Wright ed., 1990).

17   *See, e.g., The Dark Side of Biotechnology: Scientific Achievements Threaten International Treaty Banning Biological Warfare,* 224 SCI. 1215 (1984); Melissa Hendricks, *Germ War: Designing Disease,* WASH. POST, Jan. 1, 1989, at B3; *Research Supported by Pentagon Stirs Germ Warfare Accusations,* N.Y. TIMES, Mar. 19, 1989, at 1.

18   The Office of the Vice Chancellor for Research is responsible for ensuring that all research conducted on the Urbana-Champaign campus of the University of Illinois complies with legal and ethical requirements concerning use of animal or human subjects. Use of animals in research is monitored through the Division of Animal Resources. Research involving human subjects is overseen by the Institutional Review Board. *See* http://www.research.uiuc.edu/.

19   Phil Handler, *Panelists Wrangle on Ethics of Professor's CIA-funded Research,* DAILY ILLINI, May 2, 1990, at 3.

20   Kelly Field, *Biosafety Committees Come Under Scrutiny,* CHRONICLE OF HIGHER EDUCATION, 29 Apr. 2005.

21   *See* SEYMOUR M. HERSH, CHEMICAL & BIOLOGICAL WARFARE 183-241 (1968); NOAM CHOMSKY ET AL, THE COLD WAR AND THE UNIVERSITY (1977).

22   Michael Scherer, *Health Warning,* MOTHER JONES, Mar. 1, 2005.

23   Brian C. Martinson, Melissa S. Anderson & Raymond de Vries, *Scientists Behaving Badly,* 435 Nature, 9 June 2005, at 737-38.

24   Biological Weapons Act of 1986 (draft implementing legislation for BWC), *reprinted in* FRANCIS A. BOYLE, THE FUTURE OF INTERNATIONAL LAW AND AMERICAN FOREIGN POLICY 299 (1989); *cf.* Biological Weapons Anti-Terrorism Act of 1989 (S. 993) (text of bill as unanimously approved Nov. 21, 1989), *reprinted in* PREVENTING A BIOLOGICAL ARMS RACE 406 (Susan Wright ed.,1990).

25   *See* http://www.gene-watch.org.

26   *See* Alan Goldstein, *Bioterror Hysteria: The New "Star Wars," at* http://www.salon.com (Dec. 9, 2003).

27   Nick Schwellenbach, *A Plague of Researchers,* BULLETIN OF ATOMIC SCIENTISTS, May/June 2005, at 14-16.

28   Eric Berger, *Biosafety Lab May Not Be As Open As Promised,* HOUSTON CHRONICLE, May 8, 2005.

29   David Francis, *More Scientists Move to Bioterror Defense Efforts,* GLOBAL SECURITY NEWSWIRE, May 13, 2005.

30   Sarah Lueck, *Bioshield Drug-Patent Plan Draws Fire*, WALL
      STREET JOURNAL, Apr. 1, 2005, at A4; *Bioshield II Legislation
      Introduced in Senate,* http://www.nti.org, Newswire Issues,
      May 3, 2005.

31   *See, e.g.,* BD. OF SCI. & EDUC., BRITISH MED. ASS'N, BIOTECHNOLOGY,
      WEAPONS AND HUMANITY II 63–71 (2004); Jonathan B. Tucker,
      *Biological Threat Assessment: Is the Cure Worse Than the
      Disease?,* ARMS CONTROL TODAY, Oct. 2004, at 13, *available at*
      http://www.armscontrol.org/act/2004_10/Tucker.asp.

32   RICK ANDERSON, HOME FRONT: THE GOVERNMENT'S WAR ON SOLDIERS 59
      (2004); JUDITH MILLER ET AL., GERMS: BIOLOGICAL WEAPONS AND AMERICA'S
      SECRET WAR 88–89 (2001).

33   *See, e.g.,* Francis A. Boyle, *Testimony in Support of S. 993,
      101st Cong., 1st Sess., The Biological Weapons Anti-Terrorism
      Act of 1989 (July 26, 1989),* in HEARING BEFORE THE SENATE COMMITTEE
      ON THE JUDICIARY, S. HRG, 101-416, Serial No. J-101-32, at 100
      (1989).

34   Biological Weapons Anti-Terrorism Act of 1989, Pub. L. No 101-
      298, 104 Stat. 201 (codified at 18 U.S.C. §§ 175–178) (1990).

35   According to http://www.usamriid.army.mil/aboutpage.htm,
      USAMRIID continues to be the lead medical research laboratory
      for the BDRP.

36   Kevin Merida & John Mintz, *Rockville Firm Shipped Germ Agents
      to Iraq, Riegle Says,* WASH. POST, Feb. 10, 1994, at A8.

37   18 U.S.C. § 175 (2004).

38   18 U.S.C. § 178 (2004).

39   Then Chairman of the U.S. Joint Chiefs of Staff General Colin
      Powell recommended the immunization program to Cheney on
      Dec. 17, 1990. JUDITH MILLER ET AL., GERMS: BIOLOGICAL WEAPONS AND
      AMERICA'S SECRET WAR 118 (2001). By Dec. 29, Powell notified
      Schwarzkopf of the decision to proceed with immediate
      inoculation of troops against anthrax and botulinum;
      immunizations began in Jan. 1991. *Id.* at 119.

40   *See generally* George J. Annas, *Mengele's Birthmark: The
      Nuremberg Code in United States Courts,* 7 J. CONTEMP. HEALTH L.
      & POL'Y 17 (1991).

41   *See generally* RICK ANDERSON, HOME FRONT: THE GOVERNMENT'S WAR
      ON SOLDIERS (2004).

42   *See* FRANCIS A. BOYLE, DESTROYING WORLD ORDER: U.S. IMPERIALISM IN
      THE MIDDLE EAST BEFORE AND AFTER SEPTEMBER 11, ch. 3 (2004).

43   *Is Military Research Hazardous to Veterans' Health? Lessons
      from World War II, the Persian Gulf, and Today: Hearing on
      H.R. 5244 Before the Senate Committee on Veterans' Affairs,*
      103d Cong. (1994), *discussed in* RICK ANDERSON, HOME FRONT: THE
      GOVERNMENT'S WAR ON SOLDIERS 112–16 (2004).

44   William J. Broad & Judith Miller, *A Nation Challenged: The
      Investigation; U.S. Recently Produced Anthrax in a Highly Lethal
      Powder Form,* N.Y. TIMES, Dec. 13, 2001, at A1.

45   *See* SEYMOUR M. HERSH, CHEMICAL & BIOLOGICAL WARFARE 72-73 (1968); Francis A. Boyle, *Bio-Warfare and Terrorism*, SYNTHESIS/ REGENERATION, Winter 2003, at 28-30.

46   BD. OF SCI. & EDUC., BRITISH MED. ASS'N, BIOTECHNOLOGY, WEAPONS AND HUMANITY II 14 (2004); COMM. ON RESEARCH STANDARDS & PRACTICES TO PREVENT THE DESTRUCTIVE APPLICATION OF BIOTECHNOLOGY, Nat'l Acad. of Scis., BIOTECHNOLOGY RESEARCH IN AN AGE OF TERRORISM 31 (2004); Barbara Hatch Rosenberg, *Allergic Reaction: Washington's Response to the BWC Protocol*, ARMS CONTROL TODAY, July/Aug. 2001, at 38, *available at* http://www.armscontrol.org/act/ 2001_07-08/rosenbergjul_aug01.asp; Mark Wheelis & Malcolm Dando, *Back to Bioweapons? The United States May Have Rejected the Bioweapons Protocol Because It Is Committed to Continuing and Expanding Its Secret Programs*, BULL. OF THE ATOMIC SCIENTISTS, Jan./Feb. 2003, at 41, 41, *available at* http:// www.thebulletin.org/. See THE BIOLOGICAL AND TOXIN WEAPONS CONVENTION WEBSITE, *at* http://www.opbw.org/ (last visited Jan. 11, 2005), for documentation relating to the successive Review Conferences of the States Parties to the BWC and other information regarding ongoing efforts to strengthen the bioweapons regime.

47   Steven M. Block, *The Growing Threat of Biological Weapons*, AMERICAN SCIENTIST, Jan.-Feb. 2004, at 28.

48   FRANCIS A. BOYLE, DESTROYING WORLD ORDER 155-56 (2004).

49   Todd S. Purdum, *A Nation Challenged: The Disease; More Checked for Anthrax; U.S. Officials Acknowledge Underestimating Mail Risks*, N.Y. TIMES, Oct. 25, 2001, at A1; William J. Broad, *A Nation Challenged: The Spores; Contradicting Some U.S. Officials, 3 Scientists Call Anthrax Powder High-Grade*, N.Y. TIMES, Oct. 25, 2001, at B6.

50   Laura Rozen, *Is a U.S. Bioweapons Scientist Behind Last Fall's Anthrax Attacks? A Growing Number of Scientific Experts Have Come to This Conclusion; But the FBI Seems Strangely Reluctant to Zero in on the Most Likely Suspects*, *at* http:// www.salon.com (Feb. 8, 2002).

51   William J. Broad et al., *A Nation Challenged: The Inquiry; Experts See F.B.I. Missteps Hampering Anthrax Inquiry*, N.Y. TIMES, Nov. 9, 2001, at A1.

52   Rick Weiss & Susan Schmidt, *Capitol Hill Anthrax Matches Army's Stocks; 5 Labs Can Trace Spores to Ft. Detrick*, WASH. POST, Dec. 16, 2001, at A1.

53   *See* Wayne Madsen, *Anthrax and the Agency: Thinking the Unthinkable*, COUNTERPUNCH, Apr. 8, 2002; Francis A. Boyle, *Biowarfare Terror Weapons and the U.S.: Home Brew?*, COUNTERPUNCH, Apr. 25, 2002.

54   *See* Laura Rozen, *The Enemy Within?*, AM. PROSPECT, May 20, 2002, at 1213, 1213, *available at* http://www.prospect.org/.

55   *See, e.g.,* Rachel Smolkin, *Into the Spotlight*, AM. JOURNALISM REV.,

Nov. 2002, at 50, *available at* http://www.ajr.org; Marilyn W. Thompson, *The Pursuit of Steven Hatfill,* WASH. POST, Sept. 14, 2003, at W6.

56   Robert O'Harrow Jr., *Six Weeks in Autumn,* WASH. POST, Oct. 27, 2002, at W6.

57   *See, e.g.,* DAVID RAY GRIFFIN, THE NEW PEARL HARBOR: DISTURBING QUESTIONS ABOUT THE BUSH ADMINISTRATION AND 9/11 (2004); MICHAEL C. RUPPERT, CROSSING THE RUBICON: THE DECLINE OF THE AMERICAN EMPIRE AT THE END OF THE AGE OF OIL (2004).

58   Richard Falk, *Foreword* to DAVID RAY GRIFFIN, THE NEW PEARL HARBOR vii (2004). The Griffin book has also been endorsed by Marcus Raskin, Howard Zinn, Rosemary Reuther, Gerry Spence, British M.P. Michael Meacher, and others.

59   DAVID RAY GRIFFIN, THE NEW PEARL HARBOR 81, 122 (2004) (footnotes omitted).

60   *See* Douglas Jehl, *Four in 9/11 Plot Are Called Tied to Qaeda in '00,* NEW YORK TIMES, Aug. 9, 2005. *See also* Patrick Martin, *9/11 Commission Told of Atta Cover-up: Intelligence Officer Goes Public in Able Danger Exposé,* WORLD SOCIALIST WEBSITE, Aug. 19, 2005, http://www.wsws.org/articles/2005/aug20-05/able-a19.shtml.

61   Bradley Graham, *War Plans Drafted to Counter Terror Attacks in U.S.: Domestic Effort is Big Shift for Military,* WASH. POST, Aug. 8, 2005.

62   Nick Schwellenbach, *Offensive Biology,* in NUCLEAR AGE PEACE FOUNDATION, A GUIDE TO THE DEMILITARIZATION OF AMERICA'S YOUTH & STUDENTS 28 (2005).

63   FRANCIS A. BOYLE, THE CRIMINALITY OF NUCLEAR DETERRENCE 162-205 (2002).

64   Ari Schuler, *Billions for Biodefense: Federal Agency Biodefense Funding,* FY2001-FY2005, 2 BIOSECURITY AND BIOTERRORISM, NO. 2, at 86-96 (2004).

65   Sarah Lueck, *Bioshield Drug – Patent Plan Draws Fire,* WALL STREET JOURNAL, April 1, 2005, at A4.

66   Office of the Press Secretary, The White House, *Remarks by the President at the Signing of S.15—Project BioShield Act of 2004,* July 21, 2004.

67   Jennifer McKee, *Lab: Bio Unit Critical,* ALBUQUERQUE JOURNAL, Nov. 11, 2001, at 1.

68   FRANCIS A. BOYLE, THE CRIMINALITY OF NUCLEAR DETERRENCE 25-26 (2002).

69   *See* FRANCIS A. BOYLE, DESTROYING WORLD ORDER 145-50 (2004).

70   FRANCIS A. BOYLE, DESTROYING WORLD ORDER 140-57 (2004).

71   ARTHUR M. SCHLESINGER, THE IMPERIAL PRESIDENCY (1973).

72   Tom Barry, *Robert "First Strike" Joseph: The Neocon of Nukes,* Counterpunch.org, June 16, 2005.

73   FRANCIS A. BOYLE, THE CRIMINALITY OF NUCLEAR DETERRENCE 136-61 (2002).

74 FRANCIS A. BOYLE, THE FUTURE OF INTERNATIONAL LAW AND AMERICAN FOREIGN POLICY 308-16 (1989).

75 JOHN W. DEAN, WORSE THAN WATERGATE (2004).

76 Marc Kaufman, *Bioterrorism Response Hampered by Problem of Profit,* WASH. POST, Aug. 7, 2005.

77 *Id.*

78 *U.S. Plans New Stockpile of Smallpox Vaccine,* WASH. POST, Aug. 17, 2005.

79 Sunshine Project, News Release, *U.S. Retains Illegal Patent on Treaty-Violating Bioweapons Grenade,* Nov. 30, 2004.

80 FRANCIS A. BOYLE, THE FUTURE OF INTERNATIONAL LAW AND AMERICAN FOREIGN POLICY 277-316 (1989). *See also* Department of Defense, Critical Technologies Plan (15 Mar. 1989); Department of Defense, Critical Technologies Plan (15 Mar. 1990).

81 *See* FRANCIS A. BOYLE, THE CRIMINALITY OF NUCLEAR DETERRENCE 36 (2002).

82 *Id.* at 136-61.

83 *See, e.g.*, Rob Stein & Shankar Vedantam, *Flu Strain Samples Remain at Large,* WASHINGTON POST, Apr. 14, 2005; *Was Deadly Flu Deliberately Sent to Laboratories?,* MSNBC News Service, Apr. 14, 2005; Lawrence K. Altman, *Test Kits Destroyed,* N.Y. TIMES, May 6, 2005 (National Briefing: Science and Health).

84 Richard S. Dunham, *A Gentleman's "C" for W,* BUSINESS WEEK, July 30, 2001. *See also If Only I Were a Dictator, by George W. Bush,* Buzzflash.com News Analysis, Oct. 29, 2002.

85 *See* Francis A. Boyle, *A Guide to Impeaching President George W. Bush,* in DESTROYING WORLD ORDER 158-72 (2004).

86 *See e.g.*, Francis A. Boyle, *Life-Science Research Faces Legal Perils,* Letter to the Editor, N.Y. TIMES, July 20, 1990; Francis A. Boyle, Letter to the Editor, 9 POLITICS & LIFE SCIENCES No. 1, at 150 (Aug. 1990); Francis A. Boyle, *Beware of BDRP,* DAILY ILLINI, July 3, 1990; Seth Shulman, *Biological Weapons: Lawyer Talks Tough,* 346 NATURE, 12 July 1990, at 95.

87 Michael C. Ruppert, *New Orleans Bioweapons and Infectious Disease Research Labs Jeopardized by Katrina,* FROM THE WILDERNESS REPORT, Sept. 13, 2005.

88 The Sverdlovsk incident was later revealed to be the tip of the iceberg for a covert, massive and illegal biowarfare program conducted by the former Soviet Union in gross violation of the BWC. *See* JEANNE GUILLEMIN, BIOLOGICAL WEAPONS 141-43 (2005).

89 *See, e.g.*, Peter Rooney, *UI Prof's Law Targets Biological War Research,* CHAMPAIGN-URBANA NEWS-GAZETTE, July 15, 1990.

Index

A

accidents 110
aerosolization 23, 24, 25, 26,
    42, 94, 95, 99, 119
Afghanistan 43, 108, 115
Agassiz, Alexander 9
Agriculture, Department of
    31, 53, 97
al-Qaeda 50, 52
American Society for Microbiology
    27
American Type Culture Collection
    (ATCC) 32, 39
anthrax 4, 6, 13, 14, 17, 30,
    39, 40, 41, 42, 44-49,
    51, 54, 55, 65, 72, 82, 89,
    96, 98, 100, 101; Ames
    strain 45-49
Anti-Ballistic Missile Systems
    Treaty (ABM Treaty) 58, 73
Ashcroft, John 17

B

Baker, Jim 33
Beasley, V.L. 122
Bhopal 89
bin Laden, Osama 51
Biological Defense Research
    Program (BDRP) 5, 24-26,
    29, 31, 33, 34, 41, 45, 60,
    87, 94, 99, 112-114, 116-
    122
biological weapons 11, 12, 17,
    19, 20, 21, 25, 34, 42,
    43, 54, 55, 56, 58, 61, 64,
    66, 68, 71, 73, 82, 88, 89,
    90, 94, 102, 115, 116
Biological Weapons Anti-Terrorism
    Act 34, 37, 42, 47, 67,
    86, 93, 94

Biological Weapons Convention
    (BWC) 5, 6, 7, 11, 14, 15,
    19-22, 24, 25, 29, 30, 31,
    32, 33, 37, 39, 41, 42, 43,
    47, 48, 54, 58, 67, 68, 73,
    75-82, 85, 86, 87, 88, 89,
    91, 94, 100, 101, 112-115,
    117, 118, 119, 121, 123,
    126-133
biological weapons research 11
BioShield Act 31, 53, 54
biowarfare laboratory 109, 110
blowback 19, 23, 59, 66
Bolton, John 14, 58, 92, 93
botulin 39, 40
Bowman, Marion "Spike" 45, 50,
    51
Buck, William 123
Bush, George H.W. 33
Bush, George W. 6, 7, 11, 17,
    18, 21, 22, 24, 27, 28,
    30, 31, 33, 34, 39, 40,
    41, 42, 43, 47, 51, 54
    61, 63, 64, 65, 66, 67, 72,
    73, 74, 77, 81, 82, 85,
    86, 88, 93, 94, 101, 106,
    108, 109, 110, 111, 113

C

Campaign for the Peaceful
    Development of the
    Biological Sciences 7, 87,
    88
Caroline Case 57
Centers for Disease Control and
    Prevention (CDC) 31, 32,
    39, 65, 95, 110
Central Intelligence Agency (CIA)
    17, 20, 26, 27, 31, 45,
    46, 47, 50, 59, 60, 71,
    96, 97, 119

Chemical and Biological Defense Program (CBDP) 6, 24, 26, 55, 59,60, 61, 62, 63, 66, 68, 71, 72, 82, 92, 93, 94, 96, 97, 98, 99, 100, 101, 102, 104, 106, 113

Chemical and Biological Warfare (CBW) Unit 21, 61, 94, 104

chemical weapons 20, 66, 67, 68, 72, 97, 114, 115, 127, 130, 131

Cheney, Richard 39, 41, 110

Civilian Defense 6, 64, 65, 66, 110

Convention on the Prohibition of the Development, Production and Stockpiling of Bacteriological (Biological) Weapons 20, 93, 126-133

Convention on the Prohibition of the Development, Production, Stockpiling and Use of Chemical Weapons 20,

Council for Responsible Genetics (CRG) 25, 29-34, 38, 45-47, 60, 68, 87, 88

D

Daschle, Tom 4, 44, 47, 49, 74

Defense Advanced Research Projects Agency (DARPA) 60, 96, 97

Defense, Department of 7, 17, 25, 53, 60, 87, 93, 94, 100, 101, 104, 113, 114, 115, 116, 118, 119, 120, 123

depleted uranium munitions 40

destructive device 70, 71

Dierks, Richard 123

DNA genetic engineering 22, 23, 24, 25, 30, 31, 38, 41

Doe, Samuel K. 119

Dugway Proving Ground 12

E

Ebright, Richard H. 30

Energy, Department of 54, 118

Environmental Protection Agency (EPA) 53, 112, 104

epidemiology 31

F

Falk, Richard 50

Federal Bureau of Investigation (FBI) 6, 17, 45, 46, 47, 48, 49, 50, 51, 52

Federation of American Scientists 46, 48

Final Programmatic Environmental Impact Statement (FPEIS) 25, 59, 60, 61, 62, 63, 82, 91-108, 113

first use 56, 61, 64, 66, 72, 82, 102, 115

Fort Detrick 4, 45, 46, 61, 63, 97, 99, 100, 106, 113

Foundation on Economic Trends 112

G

gene-splicing 22, 23

genetic-engineered micro-organisms (GEMs) 11, 94, 96, 97, 119, 120

genetically modified food 30

Geneva Protocol 21, 81, 82, 84, 124-126, 127

Gulf War I 40, 41

Gulf War II 41

Gulf War Syndrome 40

H

Harvard Divinity School 15, 45

Health and Human Services, Department of 53, 105

Hersh, Seymour 63

Hiroshima 53, 54

HIV/AIDS 13, 64, 90

Homeland Security, Department of 31, 53, 109, 110

Huet-Vaughn, Yolanda 41

Hussein, Saddam 32, 34, 39, 40

I

International Criminal Court 43
Iran 32, 40, 72
Iraq 6, 32, 33, 34, 39, 40, 43,
        56, 72, 108
Iraq-Iran War 32

J

Jakobsson, Eric 123
Joseph, Robert 58
Justice, Department of 17

K

Kellogg-Briand Peace Pact 57
King, Jonathan 4, 5, 14, 45

L

Leahy, Patrick 47, 49
Lewontin, Richard 9
Liberia 119
Liebman, Judith 123

M

Manhattan Project 53, 54
Massachusetts Institute of
        Technology (MIT) 45
McVeigh, Timothy 45
moonsuit 44, 46
Moussaoui, Zacarias 50, 51

N

Nagasaki 53, 54
National Environmental Policy Act
        (NEPA) 92, 93, 96, 102,
        103, 104, 112
National Institutes of Health (NIH)
        27, 95, 118
National Science Foundation 53
National Security Council (NSC)
        50, 58
National Security Directive
        62, 101, 106
National Security Strategy 56, 58
National Strategy for Biodefense
        58

National Strategy to Combat
        Weapons of Mass Destruc-
        tion 56, 58
Neo-Conservatives 5, 21, 22,
        24, 29, 32, 33, 34, 39, 40,
        41, 42, 43, 47, 55, 56,
        58, 59, 60, 61, 63, 72,
        73, 74, 109, 111, 112, 113
New York Times 41, 44, 45, 51
Nixon, Richard 11, 19, 20, 21,
        22, 33, 63
North Korea 72
Nuclear Non-Proliferation Treaty
        (NPT) 19, 66
nuclear weapons 19, 54, 55,
        67, 115, 118
Nuremberg Code on Medical
        Experimentation 6, 39,
        40, 41, 97
Nuremberg Tribunal 57

P

Pan-American Health Organization
        120
Patriot Act 17, 49
Pentagon 6, 21, 24, 25, 26,
        27, 29, 31, 33, 34, 40,
        41, 42, 45, 46, 47, 50, 52,
        54, 55, 58, 59, 60, 61, 68,
        71, 82, 92, 99, 102, 106,
        109, 112, 113
Plum Island 12
Powell, Colin 41
preventive warfare 56, 57, 94,
        110
Project BioShield 12, 31, 53
Project for a New American
        Century (PNAC) 6, 55, 56

R

Reagan, Ronald 5, 21, 22, 31,
        32, 39, 40, 58, 60, 61,
        73, 112, 113, 114
Rockefeller, Jay 41
Rosenberg, Barbara 46, 48
Rowley, Coleen 51
Rumsfeld, Donald 17

Rutgers 30

S

SARS 13, 90
Schlesinger, Arthur J. 57
Schwarzkopf, Norman 41
September 11 17, 55, 109
smallpox 48, 54, 65
Souris, JoLane 61, 62, 63, 104,
    105, 106, 107
State, Department of 53
Strauss, Bernard 9
Strauss, Lorna 9
Sunshine Project 71
Sverdlovsk incident 100, 115

T

Tenet, George 17
terrorism 1, 3, 4, 5, 6, 13, 14,
    17, 18, 29, 30, 31, 33,
    34, 37, 42, 44, 45, 46,
    47, 48, 49, 50, 51, 52,
    54, 55, 64, 65, 67, 68,
    72, 73, 74, 82, 86, 88,
    89, 90, 93, 94, 100, 101,
    113
Three Mile Island 89
toxin 14, 20, 30, 32, 34, 35,
    36, 37, 39, 40, 70, 77,
    82, 84, 87, 88, 96, 98, 101,
    102, 107, 115, 116, 117,
    121, 123, 127, 128, 130
Trammel, Harold 122
transparency 14, 89
tricothecene mycotoxin 116
tuberculosis 13, 89
tularemia 13

U

U.S. Army 41, 61, 96, 97, 105,
    113, 122
U.S. Army Medical Research and
    Material Command
    (USAMRMC) 61, 62,
    63, 105, 106, 113, 122
U.S. Army Medical Research

Institute of Infectious
    Diseases (USAMRIID) 96,
    97
United Nations 72, 79, 80, 81,
    82, 83, 84, 85, 102, 127,
    129, 131, 132 United
    Nations Charter 58, 79,
    80, 81, 83, 84, 85, 108,
    127, 129, 132 General
    Assembly 72, 81, 85, 127
    Security Council 50, 58,
    72, 79, 80, 81, 82, 83,
    84, 85, 129, 131
Uniting for Peace Resolution 85
University of Chicago 9
University of Illinois 5, 26, 27,
    93, 113, 116, 117, 121, 122

V

vaccines 11, 12, 15, 16, 23,
    25, 39, 40, 41, 48, 54,
    64, 65, 88, 90, 95, 97, 98
vector 37, 70
Vienna Convention of the Law of
    Treaties 75

W

Wagner 122
Weapons of Mass Destruction
    (WMD) 6, 19, 22. 42, 43,
    54, 55, 56, 57, 58, 66,
    68, 72, 76, 94, 99, 102,
    126, 127
Weir, Morton 123
Wellstone, Paul 49
Wistar Institute 120
Wolfowitz, Paul 55, 56, 59
World War II 19, 53, 57

Y

yellow rain 115, 116

Made in the USA
Coppell, TX
05 May 2021

55088628R00079